TABLE OF CONTENTS

INTRODUCTION

This book will offend some people. That fact says a lot about our society, not all of it good. There is an abundance of information and assistance available to the custodial parent attempting to collect child support.

Every state has an agency devoted exclusively to the purpose of establishing paternity, and collecting support. If the service is not free, there is only a minimal cost.

Search the internet, and you will find a plethora of books and web-sites intended to assist the parent or child seeking to collect support. You will also find private collection agencies and law firms, offering their service for profit on a contingency fee basis. Catering to those who have lost patience with slow or inefficient state agencies, they take a large share of any support eventually collected.

What you will not find, is help for the party expected to write the checks. There are several reasons for this. The first is the interests and objectives of state and federal government. They are often in

2

the position of paying substantial benefits to the children of single parents, and looking for somebody to cover the losses.

The second is a prevailing cultural stereotype, that of the "deadbeat dad." A man accused of paternity is treated with greater disdain than any criminal defendant. He can expect to encounter hostile social workers, and an openly partisan court system.

He will receive little or no useful advice, and instead be pressured to take actions against his interest for the sake of the mother and the state.

Unfortunately, as is so often the case with stereotypes, the term "dead beat dad" causes real harm to fathers, and by extension, their children. For the sake of expediency, the system frequently turns a deaf ear to men with legitimate concerns. These frequently include the legitimacy of the paternity allegation, or the financial survival of themselves or other dependents.

You have a moral responsibility to support your child. This book is in no way intended to encourage you to circumvent that responsibility. I strongly suggest that you provide for your children in every possible way, financially and otherwise. The benefits of doing so are incalculable.

However, an accused father has no obligation to fall on his sword and submit to the justice of an often unfair and arbitrary court system. The defendant in a child support case also has an obligation to himself, to see that he is treated fairly. After all, once he is ordered to pay child support, he is subject to enforcement powers up to and including imprisonment should he refuse, or be unable to pay.

This goal of this book is to provide you with all of the information you need to make informed decisions. You will first learn about paternity testing, and when and how to go about obtaining a test.

We will then discuss the process by which a child support order is established. This will include information about how child support is calculated, and what financial information is essential for you to provide to the Court. This will allow you to insure that the obligation is calculated in a manner fair to you.

Finally, we will the long term management of a child support obligation. Since child support is usually paid for many years, it is common to expect several trips to court over that period of time, even in the best case scenario. An understanding of how to request a reduction in the payment, an emergency suspension of the obligation, and how to end the obligation, is essential.

There is a glossary, which provides a summary of each state's law on child support and parentage. This area of the book also references to various sources for updated or additional information.

CHAPTER ONE

Paternity

Recently, the Federal Office of Child Support Enforcement completed a survey of men who refused to pay child support. The purpose was to determine their reasons. Surprisingly, twelve percent of the men said that the child was not theirs. (Source, Federal Office of Child Support Enforcement on their website.)

Of course, in some cases, this can be written off as mere wishful thinking. However, it is logical to assume that many are telling the truth. There are tremendous financial incentives to tie a support obligation to a man who can pay. Furthermore, because the payment is proportionate to the income of the father, there is an incentive to pick and choose among competing candidates. In other words, if you have a high income, the mother has an incentive to look to you first.

Any attorney who practices regularly in the field has a first person horror story of this sort. The one that comes to my mind involved a professional chef with a twelve year old son. When his girlfriend told him she was pregnant, he did what he considered to be "the right thing." He admitted to paternity, to avoid embarrassing her and the family. He then undertook a substantial child support obligation, and resolved to be the best father he could. This was particularly difficult, in that he had married since his relationship with the mother ended, and the two women disliked each other intensely.

This all went reasonably well for several years, until the child reached the age of twelve. That year, his aunt attended a Christmas party also attended by the mother. The mother, who was said to be drinking too much, told the aunt 'he's a big dummy. That's not his son!"

This is how I came into the picture. After several months, we obtained a Court Order for a paternity test. About three weeks later, there was conclusive proof that the child was not his.

That, however, was not the end of it. The state social services agency took the position that my client's consent to paternity was irrevocable, in spite of the fraud by the mother, and the conclusive proof to the contrary. As I learned, there is substantial authority to

7

the effect that an acknowledgement of paternity cannot be subsequently challenged, regardless of circumstance.

In the end, the Court did the right thing. The court reversed the adjudication of paternity, and cancelled the child support obligation. It was, at best, a hollow victory.

My client was initially pleased with the result, and happy to have obtained a measure of justice. He asked me about the possibility of suing the mother the recover his twelve years of fraudulently obtained payments.

Unfortunately, since the mother was unemployed, there was no real possibility of her paying him back. Despite his tremendous loss, I advised him not to throw good money out for bad.

The saddest part of the story was the effect on the child. My client attempted to maintain his relationship with him, but was not successful. The child was understandably devastated by these events, with predictably negative consequences to his life.

There is a lesson to be learned here. If there is any doubt whatsoever about the paternity issue, demand a paternity test

8

immediately. This is for your own protection, and that of the child. Do not sign an acknowledgement of paternity without definitive proof.

The good news is that, if you follow this advice, the Court has no choice but to honor your request. The United States Supreme Court, in the case of **Little v. Streeter, 452 U.S. 1, 101 S.C. 2202, 68 L.Ed.2d 627 (1985),** resolved the issue definitively.

In **Streeter**, the Court held that under the Fourteenth Amendment of the United States Constitution, the defendant in a paternity suit had a right to be heard. Absent an informed and appropriate waiver, this meant that the state could not deny the putative father blood grouping tests. This was true even if he was indigent, and could not otherwise afford them.

This ruling is the cornerstone to a meaningful defense in a paternity action. . However, it is also essential to understand, despite representations to the contrary, the testing process is subject to human error. .

9

This is inherent in the nature of the process. DNA testing refers to the process of examining an individual's DNA markers for the purpose of genetic human identification, thereby determining the relationship between two people.

This is accomplished through direct examination of the genetic material that the child inherited from the biological parents. DNA is located throughout the human body, in the same identical form. The DNA in the bloodstream is the same as that in the skin, lining of the cheek, muscle, bone, teeth, and various other tissues.

In paternity testing, the genetic characteristics of the child are first compared with to those of his or her mother. Those characteristics of the child that cannot be found in the mother will logically have been inherited from the natural father.

The next step is to obtain genetic material from the father. If the subject man does not have the genetic characteristics necessary to be the biological father, he must be excluded. If, on the other hand, his DNA does contain those genetic characteristics, then the probability that he is the true biological father is calculated and reported by the laboratory.

The sample is commonly taken using a buccal swab. This is a specialized applicator with a sponge, cotton, or Dacron tip. The applicator is simply rubbed on the inside of the cheek to collect epithelial cells. The process is equally effective to a blood sample, considerably safer, and painless.

From the point of view of the putative father, there is really no way to "trick' the test. The DNA material cannot be altered by any behavior on the part of the putative father. Medication, alcohol, food, drugs, or lifestyle cannot alter DNA patterns within an individual at all.

The testing agencies long ago put in place measures to prevent a putative father from sending in a "ringer." Typically, the mother, child, and putative father will be scheduled to provide samples at the same time. When this is impossible, a picture ID will be required, and a copy will be placed in the file.

However, it is surprisingly easy for the lab to make a mistake. This is a fact either ignored or unappreciated by Judges, who accept the test results as indisputable.

11

A recent **Washington Post** article reflects much of the truth. The article, dated August 21, 2005, is entitled "Paternity Suit Raises Doubts about DNA Tests." It reveals much about the harried, fast food atmosphere in which these tests are performed.

In the case, the alleged father testified that he had stopped seeing the mother years before she gave birth. He did the smart thing, and demanded a paternity test. Under the circumstances, he assumed that his problem would be over in short order.

The paternity testing was performed by Laboratory, Corp. of America, one of the largest paternity testers in the country. At the time, Laboratory Corp. was the exclusive contractor for the state of Virginia, where the case was litigated.

The test resulted in a two page report which concluded that the probability of paternity was ninety nine percent. The putative father was stunned. He hired an attorney and commenced a legal battle which would last for two years.

In the end, a Fairfax County, Virginia Judge ruled that the state had failed to adequately prove paternity. The Judge's comments are telling:

"I thought LabCorp's performance was shoddy," Stitt said at a hearing in May after ruling that the state did not prove Chreky was the father. "I think something unfair happened in this case, where a citizen was put to the greatest extent to defend himself against what really has turned out to be a moving target as far as where LabCorp is concerned...I'm concerned about what level of oversight is being exercised by the commonwealth of LabCorp's work."

The testimony in the case revealed that LabCorp performed more than one hundred thousand DNA paternity tests for public and private interests every year. Astoundingly, it was revealed that the company had only **five** employees to review the data and making paternity determinations. One supervisor testified that he issued an average of one paternity report every four minutes during a ten hour shift.

By all indications, the caseworkers and judicial officers who make these decisions are blissfully unaware of this. Yet, the fact remains that these tests are administered by human beings, who are prone to error. These harried, overworked employees collect,

13

label, store, read, and analyze huge amounts of data. It is entirely reasonable that the results be subject to scrutiny, as DNA is in other areas of litigation.

The article concludes with a statement by Laurence B. Mueller, an evolutionary biology professor at the University of California-Irvine. He had been tracking laboratory errors in DNA cases for several years. Mueller notes that DNA labs "use techniques that have been automated, like Hostess Twinkies, on an assembly line." Most of the time, the Twinkies are fine. But once in a while, you get a bad one." (See **The Washington Post, "Paternity Suit Raises Doubts About DNA Tests,"** Tom Jackman, Author, August 21, 2005)

So what can you do to protect yourself? First of all, be aware of some of the more common potential areas for problems. For example, where there are two or more putative fathers who are related (i.e. brothers, fathers, father and son, etc.), DNA testing presents unique challenges.

In such cases, additional testing is required, and all related alleged fathers must be tested together to obtain conclusive results.

14

Despite this, it is common for laboratories not to even ask subjects about this possibility. A review of applicable case law reveals that this issue has seldom, if ever, been raised as a legal defense in an adjudication of paternity.

There is always a risk of a sample not containing enough DNA for the test. This can occur for several reasons, including collection error, dry mouth, or excessive tobacco usage. This error is ordinarily being acknowledged, and an additional sample obtained.

There is also the possibility that the sample shows a "single exclusion", which might or might not be a mutational error. The distinction is crucial. When just one of the DNA systems examined reveals a mismatch between the alleged father and child, it is called a single exclusion. At this stage, the laboratory cannot conclude paternity or non-paternity without further testing.

Further testing might reveal more exclusionary DNA systems, thus eliminating the subject as a putative father. Alternately, the further testing might reveal more matching DNA systems. In this case, the laboratory might deem the mismatch to be a "mutational event," a naturally occurring, single exclusion which does not disprove paternity.

If there are at least two exclusionary DNA systems between the subject and the child, this is called a double exclusion. In this case, it is highly unlikely that the laboratory will issue a positive finding as to paternity.

However, if the two exclusionary systems reveal data that are only one number apart, there remains a remote possibility that a **double** mutational event has occurred. While this is extremely rare, additional testing should be done to provide a conclusive result.

Unfortunately, it is difficult, if not impossible, to determine whether good faith errors have been made in the identification and transfer of data. The best that can be done is to expose for the Court the inherent flaws in the process, and presents factual testimony that would raise doubt as to the conclusiveness of the test.

Certain evidence is obviously most compelling. For example, a credible witness as to the impossibility of paternity might turn the tide. If medical evidence exists of impotence at the time of conception, this should be obtained well before a hearing, and presented at trial. Likewise, if there is credible evidence that the alleged father never had intercourse with the mother, or ceased doing so well before the probable time of conception, this will be crucial.

To insure that such evidence is heard, it is essential to understand applicable state law. The appendix of this book addresses state law as to several topics related to paternity.

The first of these is the issue of presumptions. In various factual circumstances, a court will presume that a man is the father of a child. The burden is then on him to prove otherwise, which can be difficult or impossible to do. The presumption is universally applicable where a man is married to the mother of the child. However, many states extend this to circumstances in which the parties are recently divorced, have co-habited, or where the man has previously acknowledged paternity in some way.

Such a presumption has a tremendous effect. As a result, a man is often given a limited period of time to file a lawsuit to

17

adjudicate the issue. If he fails to do so, he is conclusively determined to be the father of the child. There might also be limitations upon what actions he can take, or evidence he can present to defend himself.

The second issue is whether the state courts address custody and visitation at a paternity hearing. The minority of states that do so are adjudicating a number of critical issues at a single, brief hearing. It is important to be aware of this.

Finally, there is a summary of the state evidence law relative to paternity hearings. In most states, evidence can be presented in alternate forms including written testimony or teleconferencing. This often requires the permission of a judge, and a certain amount of advance planning.

It is essential to remember that, to almost all Judges, the tests results are stone pillars of truth. They are virtually beyond attack, except by medical evidence to the contrary, or other, highly compelling proof. It will seldom be found in the testimony of the putative father alone, which will be discounted as unreliable on the basis of self interest.

18

So, what about the possibility of outright fraud, of being framed? In my experience, conspiracies are exceedingly rare. When present, proving their existence is something like nailing jello to a wall. However, they doubtless do occur.

In **Rivera v. Minnich, 1987 S.CT. 2906, 483 U.S. 574, 107 S.CT. 3001, 97 L.Ed.2d 473, 55 U.S.L.W. 5075,** the United States Supreme Court concedes as much:

> "...in the field of contested paternity...the truth is so often obscured because social pressures create a conspiracy of silence or, worse, induce deliberate falsity. The person alleged to be the father has a legitimate interest in not being declared the father of a child he had no hand in bringing into the world. It is important to him that he not be required to provide support and direct financial assistance to one not his child"

There are other things that can be done when tests results are suspect. For example, it is possible to petition the Court for a second paternity test, performed by an independent laboratory. This request is frequently denied, but at worst, provides additional grounds for an appeal.

It might be useful to scrutinize the circumstances under which the tests were performed, by bringing laboratory employees to testify at trial. This would allow for the opportunity to challenge the reliability of the process, as was done in the Virginia case discussed earlier in the chapter.

The issue of chain of custody of test samples should be closely examined. This relates to who handled the DNA materials in question, where they were stored, and who had access to them at various times. Since a paternity action is a quasi-criminal matter, it is appropriate to raise the issue of whether tainting or tampering with the sample could have occurred. These evidentiary issues are addressed later in later, in the Chapter "**A Little Basic Evidence Law**."

These are complex trial issues, which present a challenge for even experienced lawyers. If resources permit, it would be wise to retain counsel in such a case. There are few other legal matters in which the expense of counsel is more justified. Consider that a very modest child support obligation of three hundred dollars per month will amount to sixty four thousand eight hundred dollars ($64,800.00) in payments over the eighteen year life of the Order.

This putative father would be unbelievably lucky. His child support obligation would have been at the very bottom on the pay scale, and remained unaltered for nearly two decades. The scenario would only be possible if the mother took an attitude of benign neglect, and there were no state agency involvement.

The typical father will pay far more. He is facing a daunting financial challenge. His own financial well being, and often that of other dependants, is at risk. In some cases, his very survival might be at stake.

To say this is not to disregard the needs of the mother and child. It is simply the other side of the story.

CHAPTER TWO

Can We Keep It Out Of Court?

Chances are that relations between you and the mother of the child are difficult at best. Otherwise, you wouldn't be reading this. However, there is a real possibility that the two of you can work cooperatively.

There are tremendous advantages to doing so. The child support enforcement system is designed in a matter adversarial to you. It is a vehicle for the expedient removal of your personal wealth, and even your freedom, should you fail to pay.

It brings forth the power of federal and state government to rigidly enforce your financial obligation. Worse, it provides only remote and conditional relief should you be unable to pay, no matter what the circumstances.

There is the chance that any consensual agreement between yourself and the mother will eventually fail. Even if it does, you are still far better off. For as long as it lasts, you can live without fearing the vengeance of a state court judge.

22

Furthermore, until a child support petition is actually filed, you are unlikely to incur any obligation to pay retroactive child support. Such Orders for "back" payment often accumulate into huge obligations, with the result being a father who spends his life in a revolving door between home and prison.

An agreement between the parents can work for both parties.

From the point of view of the mother, there is also considerable appeal in staying out of the system. Many mothers intuitively understand the importance of the relationship between the father and their child. They also understand how difficult it is to cultivate that relationship through an adversarial system with harsh enforcement tactics. Such mothers are willing to negotiate, within reason.

If she puts the interest of the child first, and respects you as a parent, there is a possibility of resolving the matter consensually. If so, you will have a simpler, fear free life, and a more flexible party to deal with in bad times.

This is not an opportunity to take advantage of the mother, and by extension, your child. If you attempt this, be honest with the mother about the financial situation, and do everything possible to arrive at a fair figure. A deal brokered through pressure tactics will inevitably collapse, usually quickly. There are far too many social workers, child advocates, and single parent friends out there, constantly offering advice, for a bad deal to hold.

Above all, if you are able to agree to a weekly, bi-weekly, or monthly sum to be paid direct to the mother, **pay as promised and pay on time.**   The mother will have no reason to file a petition for Court ordered support, if she trusts that the underlying obligation will be honored. If the child has unusual or emergency needs, step up and pay your fair share. Keep in mind that the typical child support order would require you to pay a percentage of medical expenses not covered by insurance.

By taking care of your child, without having to be held up at gun point, you will earn the respect of the mother, your child, and others. You also receive the immeasurable benefits of not being acquainted with the local social services workers and family court judges.

The agreement should be in writing, and drawn up cooperatively between yourself and the mother. This is your opportunity to discuss the particulars before it is signed, and thereby commit the mother to the agreement. It should, at a minimum, be specific as to these details:

- The full names, and mailing addresses, of each parent
- The full name, and date of birth, of the child
- The agreed upon amount of payment
- The payment schedule, weekly, bi-weekly, or monthly
- The date of the first payment
- A method for payment, check, certified check, or other
- The notarized signatures of both parties

This is also an opportunity to discuss the issues of joint or split custody, or a specific visitation schedule. When considering these points, a key question is whether you are interested in ever obtaining full or joint-custody of the child.

While the topic is beyond the scope of this book, you should be aware of certain important points. The first is that, like the child support provisions, your voluntary agreement

25

ROBERT W. RUSHING JR.

regarding access to the child is not enforceable in Court. An agreement executed by the two of you without court approval, is essentially a handshake deal with the mother. As such, until and unless it is approved by a Judge and incorporated into an Order, no one will lift a finger to enforce your right to see your child.

The second is that, inevitably, most of these agreements fail. Sometimes, this happens when the mother remarries or enters into another significant relationship. The new man in the house often resents the father, and wishes to limit his presence in the home.

Whatever the reason, when it happens, it can be ugly. You should always be taking certain common sense measures to protect yourself, since you are likely to have to litigate these issues, after all. Expect your best efforts and intentions to be scrutinized and mischaracterized.

The following are good habits to maintain until you drop your child off at college:

Copyright © 2010 Robert W. Rushing, Jr. All rights reserved.

- Keep all receipts, checks, and any evidence of payment

- Keep a calendar of all visitation exercised with the child

- Keep a record of all requests for visitation that are denied

- Keep receipts for any benefits to the child paid beyond set support

- Cultivate communication with the mother through e-mail, and keep copies of all e-mails regarding issues related to the child.

These records should be kept in the same manner as old tax returns. Keep the files for a period of at least seven years. The documentation could be priceless if your relationship with the mother ever deteriorates.

There are a couple of other key points to discuss as to informal agreements. In such situations, by opting out of the court system, you and the mother are depriving yourself of an all powerful, third party decision maker. Since there is no Judge, communication becomes all the more essential.

If you are unable to pay the agreed upon support, explain this fact and the reason for your inability to pay immediately. Pay as close to the agreed upon amount as possible, and as consistently with the payment schedule as possible. Even if the mother decides to file a petition for support, your good faith effort to communicate and abide by the agreement should influence the Judge in your favor.

There is a final issue which must be addressed as to this topic. This issue frequently breaks down good working arrangements between parents, and causes repercussions well beyond the parental situation. This is the issue of who takes the tax deduction as to the dependent child.

First of all, it should be understood that the deduction ordinarily belongs to the custodial parent. However, the custodial parent can convey the deduction over to the non-custodial parent by agreement. If the mother is unemployed, or has a limited income, this is probably a reasonable request.

However, such a conveyance should be executed in writing by the mother, and kept in the permanent records of the father. I

28

strongly suggest that a professional accountant or tax preparer prepare the documentation of this agreement.

Under no circumstances do I suggest simply taking the deduction, without discussing the issue with the mother. This invites the possibility of family court litigation, and additionally, of triggering state and federal tax audits.

If the incomes are comparable, many parents agree to divide the deduction in some equitable manner. I have seen parents successfully abide by an agreement which provided that one parent take the deduction on even numbered years, and the other on odd numbered years. I have also seen parents split up the deductions as to multiple children.

A well executed, and reliably performed consensual agreement has advantages that no Court Order can provide. This is a highly desirable alternative for parents capable of working together cooperatively.

CHAPTER THREE

How Child Support is Calculated

The child support system is, in many ways, different from what you might expect. Most defendants enter into the process with serious misconceptions as to procedure and law. This often leads to disastrous results in court.

Still, you don't need a crash course in civil procedure and an accounting degree to protect yourself. You just need to understand what facts and figures are important to the calculation. This will allow you to make the most persuasive argument.

The most crucial of these are gross income and net income. There are countless technical definitions for these terms. However, the best description I ever heard was given to me by a tax preparer. "Gross income," he said, "is what you **think** you earn. Net income is what you actually take home after the government carves up your paycheck."

If you or the mother happen to be self employed, things get harder. The child support guidelines of most states will define gross

30

income, and will usually include money, property, or other services from most sources. In other words, non-monetary compensation will be included in your income.

The definition is usually comparable to the one used by the Internal Revenue Service. If you prepare your own tax return, you understand how broadly the government defines income. That experience is relevant here.

The child support obligation is calculated based primarily upon the gross or net incomes of the two parents. In certain states, the figure is determined by simply taking the income of the non-custodial parent, and assigning a percentage of that income to child support. This is called the *Percentage of Income Model.*

This brings us to the first major misconception as to how child support is calculated. Most people assume that the method of calculating child support is fairly consistent from state to state. The truth is that the methods of calculation vary considerably. As such, the amount of support you pay might be substantially higher or lower depending upon nothing more than where you live.

31

Even among the states using the *Income Percentage Model*, there are differences in application. For example, some states simply use a fixed percentage of the non-custodial parent's income. In other states, the percentage increases with the income of the non-custodial parent.

There is only one reliable way to know what is considered "gross income" in your state. That is to be familiar with your state child support guidelines. The guidelines are not only subject to change, but are automatically reviewed and modified periodically in most states. As such, it is important to verify that you are working from a current set of your state child support guidelines.

The appendix to this book includes a page devoted to the child support system of each state. This is a useful starting point to familiarize yourself with your state's law. Keep in mind that the information included is subject to change following the date of publication.

In general, the following things are considered to be "gross income" in most states:

1. salaries;

2. wages;

3. commissions;

4. bonuses;

5. dividends;

6. pensions;

7. trust income;

8. annuities;

9. social security benefits;

10. worker's compensation benefits;

11. certain personal injury settlements;

12. unemployment insurance benefits;

13. disability payments;

14. scholarships;

15. educational grants;

16. barter, or services received in exchange for services;

17. certain judgments;

18. goods received in exchange for services;

19. prizes;

20. certain gifts

When in doubt, keep two factors in mind. Firstly, examine your tax return. If the item is listed as income for Federal income tax purposes, it is almost certainly income for this purpose. The information on the return will be considered an admission by the judge, who will readily include the item in your gross income.

Secondly, assume that the custodial parent or the state agency will probably obtain a copy of your tax return. It is comparatively simple for a state agency to obtain the return, and to do so is often standard operating procedure.   If you are self employed, or the extent of your income is in question, expect this to happen.

If you substantial benefits from your work other than wages or salaries, you should consider obtaining the services of a certified public accountant. The expense is a relative bargain in allowing you to be present credible evidence as to these issues, and thereby avoid being saddled with an unfair and unrealistic child support payment.

You should carefully consider whether each such benefit is properly included in your gross income. If the item in question is not listed in the state statutes or regulations, you have a legitimate argument.

Furthermore, you should consider the nature of the benefit, and the reason by which it is provided. These may lead to an argument as to fairness. For example, a scholarship if often based upon the limited financial means of the recipient, and provides a long term benefit to any dependant.

The effect of including the scholarship in the income of the non-custodial parent for the purpose of calculating child support is to hinder him in pursuing his education. This, in the long run, harms all who look to him for financial support.

There are three arguments which can persuade a Judge to exclude a non-monetary benefit from gross income. The most frequently successful is any benefit to the child who is the subject of the support action. It is a logical and comfortable step for a Judge to conclude that it makes good sense to withhold a smaller short term benefit from the dependant child to increase the long term earning

35

potential of the non-custodial parent. A scholarship is the perfect example of this.

The second argument is hardship to other dependents. When raising this argument, you may get a predictable initial response. You will be told that you should have considered the problem earlier, before remarrying, having another child, etc.

You respond by defending your prior good judgment. A stable employment history, or a hard financial hardship beyond your control, is often persuasive. It is also important to point out any major financial obligations which involve compelling need, such as medical expenses, or are not negotiable, such as tax liens.

The final argument relates to circumstances which cause short term disruption to income. These situations often include injury or illness, which results in a disability, worker's compensation, or personal injury claim.

The nature of the compensation you receive is crucial in such cases. The money you get might be intended to replace lost wages, compensate for the loss of property, or be based upon permanent injury or disability.

If the payment is described as compensation for lost wages, it is a part of gross income for purposes of calculating income tax and child support. If, on the other hand, the payment is in compensation of medical bills, based upon permanent disability, or for loss of property, it is arguably not a part of your gross income. The documents you sign to settle a case will address this issue, as they must for tax purposes.

The odds are that the attorney representing you in the personal injury case is not involved in your child support case. It is important that you point out to him or her that the characterization of the proceeds of your settlement is important to you.

The attorney cannot falsify or deliberately mischaracterize the basis of your compensation. However, there are frequently shades of grey as to this issue, and it might be ethical and appropriate to characterize the payments in a way that benefits you. It is wise to raise this issue early in the settlement process.

37

Of course, if the settlement documents support your position, bring them to Court. There is nothing more suspicious to a Judge than testimony about the contents of paperwork which is not available to the Court.

There is a final issue concerning gross income which should be addressed. This is the possibility that the Court finds that the non-custodial parent is deliberately holding down his earning capacity to avoid paying child support. In such cases, the Court may calculate support based upon *attributed income.*

The argument is essentially this. Your physical health, work history, and education argue that you could be working more, or paid more. Particularly if there is a recent job change, or decrease in hours or wages, you are suspect.

If the Court concludes that you are manipulating your income to avoid paying support, the result can be disastrous. The Court can simply calculate the child support obligation based upon your earning *potential.* Too often, Judges wrongfully jump to this conclusion, resulting in an unreasonable support obligation that the non-custodial parent cannot meet.

38

If you anticipate such a problem, come prepared. If you are suffering from a short term lack of hours at work, bring along a statement from your employer addressing the situation. If your current job pays less than your previous one, bring proof of the reasons for change. If possible, also bring proof of your efforts to obtain a better paying job.

The decision to attribute income to a non-custodial parent is primarily based upon a finding that he is acting in bad faith. A conclusion as to state of mind is certainly more subject to challenge than a simple calculation of numbers. Therefore, there is at least the possibility of a successful appeal. .

If you find yourself on the losing end of such an Order, consult an attorney immediately. The deadlines for filing and perfecting an appeal vary from state to state, but are notoriously short. Although appellate litigation always involves substantial costs, enough money is usually at stake in a child support case to justify the expense.

In many states, certain items are always deducted from gross income. These will be specified in the forms used to complete the computations, and are hard to miss. For example, in my home state

39

ROBERT W. RUSHING JR.

of South Carolina, the following items are invariably exempt from gross income.

- Federal taxes

- State taxes

- Health insurance applicable to the child or children through a prior child support obligation

Essentially, the same rules apply as to documenting the nature of an expense. It is important to bring along check stubs, receipts, or records, which will indicates the amounts spent and the purpose.

The health insurance issue can present more difficulty. It is often impossible to look at your paycheck and determine how much of your health insurance expense is attributable to your child. This will require a visit to the human resources department of your employer, or a call to the insurer. Be sure to get written documentation of the figure they provide.

For the self employed, determination of gross income is much more complicated. The owner of a business will frequently go through a complex, lengthy hearing, not unlike a tax audit. The

Copyright © 2010 Robert W. Rushing, Jr. All rights reserved.

issues can range from the extent and legitimacy of business expenses, to the existence or extent of profit, to the possibility that the books are "cooked" or fraudulent.

The wisest course is to treat the hearing like an audit. If possible, bring along receipts or other documentation of all major expenses. Expect more scrutiny if your business is losing money, particularly if your lifestyle does not reflect hardship.

If you have not already done so, consider incorporating your business. The cost is minimal, and a true bargain relative to the benefits. Besides considerable liability protection, this arrangement allows you to y set up your own salary and compensation plan.

This is because of the fact that a corporation is considered an entirely separate individual with an existence of its own. The corporation you "father" by paying a small fee and filing a few papers with the state can file its own tax returns, enter into contracts, sue and be sued, and even be prosecuted for crimes.

Better yet, it can earn its own income, which is not subject to your child support obligation. This does not prevent a Judge from

41

"attributing' all or a part of that income to you. Nevertheless, the income of the corporation is not your own, until the corporation pays out compensation to you.

If you have already set your business up as a corporation, or intend to do so, avoid overreaching. By this, I mean use your common sense, and resist the urge to set up your finances to circumvent legitimate financial obligations.

It is perfectly acceptable to set up a salary for yourself, and use the corporation to obtain tax free benefits such as a company car. However, the non-custodial parent with a successful business, and shows evidence of an affluent lifestyle, is better off to declare his legitimate income. The alternative approach results in the same sort of credibility problems experienced by a drug dealer in a two thousand dollar suit.

This is an area of the law in which it is bad idea to go cheap. It is simple enough to file papers with the secretary of state, and create your own corporation. It is also not that difficult to keep up with the required filings for tax returns and other purposes.

However, if you have substantial income from a business, the price of a competent attorney or certified public accountant is money well spent. Their expertise will allow you to maximize the benefits of the corporate structure, and avoid mistakes.

A number of states use a slightly more complicated method to calculate support. It is sometimes called the *Combined Income Model.* This is the method employed in my home state of South Carolina.

In these states, the income of both parents is combined into a total income, as though the two were cohabiting in a household. This figure can then be used in several ways.

Using my own home state as an example, the incomes of the parents are combined. This figure is used to determine an amount of money which would be expected to be used in support of the child or children.

The South Carolina child support guidelines reference to a chart from which this figure is derived. The obligation for the total

43

amount is then divided between the two parents, based upon their relative percentage of the combined income.

The formula also takes into account certain expenses paid on behalf of the minor child. These often include day care and medical insurance. The expenses are deducted from the income share of the parent who pays them.

If the parents have a joint or shared custody arrangement, the formula will adjust the payment accordingly. This is based upon the fact that the parents are either raising the child as equal partners, or the non-custodial parent is already spending far more on the child than would usually be the case. .

The South Carolina model does take into account certain other factors. The existence of a prior support obligation for another child will usually be a basis for reduction.

The guidelines also allow some discretion on the part of the Court based upon hardship. However, in my experience, convincing a Family Court Judge to deviate substantially from the guidelines is an uphill battle. It might be worthwhile or necessary to try, but the chances of success are slim.

In general, the process can be summarized as follows:

A. Determine the gross income of the father.

B. Determine the gross income of the mother.

C.   Determine the total income amount from your state guidelines.

D.   Adjust for any deductions from the income of father or mother.

E.   Adjust for any additions to the income of father or mother.

F.   Calculate the proportionate share of income due from each parent.

G. Add any court costs or administrative costs.

Once you understand the process, your purpose is clear. **You must appear at your hearing with a complete understanding of your financial situation, including income and expenses.**

Furthermore, you must appear with appropriate documentation available for the Court. Particularly if you intend to represent yourself at the hearing, there is nothing that engenders more goodwill from a Judge than a well thought out case with organized trial exhibits.

Of course, this is only half of the battle. Depending on the circumstances, you might or might not have a great deal of familiarity with the financial situation of the mother.

It is helpful that, in most states, the financial disclosure forms used at the hearing are sworn documents, like tax returns. Although it is seldom done, there is every legal basis to prosecute a parent who misrepresents his or her income for perjury.

To protect yourself, it is first necessary to be sure the custodial parent or state agency presents its evidence in a proper form. By this, I mean that you must insist on a sworn document verifying the extent of her income and all relevant expenses.

I have frequently seen social workers or attorneys present check stubs instead of verified documents, or informally advise the Court as to income and expenses.

If this is permitted, the mother is effectively off the hook as to the perjury issue. If the Court appears inclined to accept oral testimony as to the relevant figures, at least insist that the mother be placed upon oath to present the evidence. You can always verify any questionable testimony at a later date.

The issue of shared custody situation presents its own problems. The fact is that child support is often ordered before the court has addressed the issue of custody. There are several reasons for this. They include the urgency placed upon the support process by the state, as well as the nature of support hearings. They are usually limited in scope, and involve "just doing the math."

As such, the parents leave the hearing with no ruling as to the custody issue, and no directive as to visitation. The mother, in

47

particular, often wrongfully assumes that she has been awarded custody because she has been awarded support. By extension, she considers herself to be in a position to dictate when, where, and whether the father sees his child.

This can cause a souring of the relationship between the parents. The mother, feeling an increased sense of control, will begin to dictate terms. This will happen as to financial issues, and those related to access to the minor child.

Worse, the Judicial system often gives credit to this unwritten and non-existent custody order. This happens when the issues of custody and visitation are finally heard in court. Because the mother is receiving child support payments, the Judge is primed to believe her claim that she is exercising sole custody of the child, whether true or not. The effect is to substantially erode the opportunity of the father to be heard.

As such, the father is forced to walk a fine line. He can attempt to address circumstances related to custody and visitation, and risk a hostile response from the Court for discussing these "irrelevant" issues. He can, alternately, limit himself to indicating that he spends

48

more time and money with the child than is customary, and ask the mother to confirm this.

The best approach is one that requires a little forethought and preparation. Keep a calendar of the time you spend with your child every week, so that you can testify as to specific dates and times. The calendar is relevant evidence in the child support hearing, provided that your state makes adjustments to the support obligation based upon joint or shared custody.

If the child spends substantial time in your home; by this I mean more than just alternating weekends, you will benefit in several ways.

First of all, you will likely receive a credit in the child support calculation based upon your greater out of pocket expense. Secondly, the order might reflect the extent of your involvement with the child, which will help to protect your right to access in the future.

The calendar will usually be considered highly credible evidence, because it is a contemporaneous document. The Judge

49

will appreciate the opportunity to review your exhibit, and be impressed by your careful record keeping..

The likely result is a reduction in the child support payment. Bring along your records and receipts, showing regular expenses of the child paid by you. This should seal the deal.

Still better, you should end up with an Order more reflective of the actual shared custody arrangement. This could be crucial at a later date, if you begin to have problems working with the mother, and decide to seek full custody of the child.

There are other limited situations in which the non-custodial parent is entitled to a reduction in the payment. These vary from state to state, another reason why it is essential to study your state child support guidelines carefully before the hearing.

It is possible that the child has some form of income of his or her own. The source might be a job, an inheritance, a trust, or the proceeds of lawsuit. Under certain circumstances, the income might entitle the non-custodial parent to a reduction in the child support obligation, or its elimination outright.

The obvious and most common case involves the child who leaves school and obtains full time employment. It is entirely reasonable to argue that he or she is no longer dependent on the custodial parent. In other words, he or she is emancipated.

Even with a part time job, it might be possible to make this argument if the income is substantial enough. However, it is wise to proceed with caution in making this argument. The fact that a sixteen year old works a few hours at a fast food restaurant is not going to get the non-custodial parent off the hook and to argue that it should looks petty and foolish.

In the case of a trust, inheritance, and lawsuit proceeds, the income is likely to be substantially more. However, there is often an additional hurdle to clear. In many cases, neither the minor nor the custodial parent has full control or even access to the funds. They are usually under the control of a trustee, or similar fiduciary.

This is another situation which might require homework on your part. If you are aware of such an income source, but unfamiliar with the circumstances, request documentation. These could include trust instruments, bank account records, or settlement documents. If

51

these cannot be obtained for the asking, a properly served subpoena will do the trick.

The flip side of the coin is the case in which the child has unusual expenses, usually medical or educational. There are two common scenarios here.

The first involves a child who is needs money to further his or her education. The states, again, vary as to when it is permissible to increase the child support obligation on this basis. They likewise differ, as we will discuss later, as to whether it is permissible to extend the period for payment of support for this purpose.

The best defense arguments as to this issue are often effective. Sadly, they are also arguments that tend to be hurtful to the child. Whether to use them is a matter of personal choice.

The first and best is an argument of fundamental fairness. There is no law in any state that requires a custodial parent to pay for a child's post graduate education. As such, it is difficult to justify requiring the non-custodial parent to do so.

They are alternative methods by which the child can obtain the money, including scholarships, students loans, and part time jobs. The law in most states puts some obligation on the student to pursue these opportunities.

There is also the cynical, though sometimes true, fact that the child might be unlikely to succeed in higher education. Awkward as this argument is, a sub-par academic record for the child might convince a Judge not to create a Court imposed college fund.

When the issue is the disability of a child, there is considerable difficulty in framing an argument. However, there is a certain advantage in that you will usually be familiar with the extent and nature of the child's medical condition.

If this is not the case, it is essential to obtain and review the documentation. It is a certainty that some medical records will be presented at the hearing. The problem is that you will likely see only a few pages of documentation, selected by the other side to.

As such, you will want to get all the medical evidence you can, as soon as possible. This can be highly difficult, in that federal law

53

substantially limits the right of access to medical records of third parties.

Often, the best source for such evidence is the custodial parent or the child. If the documents cannot be obtained voluntarily, it is usually possible to obtain them through a subpoena. Keep in mind that hospitals and doctors are used to charging high fees for accessing and copying their records, that will often be passed on to you as an expense of complying with the subpoena.

If your relationship with the mother permits, you might simply ask her, or her attorney for the records. Well before the hearing; send a written request for any and all medical evidence to be presented at trial. Keep a copy of the letter for your records, and bring it to the hearing.

Also request the names, addresses, and treatment dates for all health care providers who have seen the child for five years. If the child has frequently changed doctors, this might be a sign that there has been disagreement as to his or her treatment or condition. Request the records for every provider, and issue a subpoena.

If the other side does not cooperate fully, ask the Court to continue the case until they do so. Be sure to bring documentation of your attempt to obtain the records well before the hearing. If possible, it is wise to make the request at least thirty days before the court date.

If you are aware that the child is seriously disabled, this course of action is unnecessary and might be seen as cruel. There is, of course, the possibility that the child is receiving income from either a private insurer or, more likely, the government. However, if the source is the federal of state government, chances are the provider is a party to the action, seeking reimbursement from you.

There is also the possibility of an adjustment in the child support obligation based upon which parent gets the federal and state income tax deductions. This is an issue which can usually be turned to the advantage of the non-custodial parent. However, it is often mishandled.

The key is to negotiate the issue beforehand, and present alternatives to the other side. Depending on her work situation and income, the mother might not want or need the deduction. Even if

55

she is employed, she might be willing to share the deductions for multiple children, or alternate the deduction in even and odd years.

The bottom line is an increase in your spendable income. The benefit comes to you at the expense of state or federal government, instead of the mother and child. As such, this might be the one scenario in this book that ends with everybody happy.

Alternately, certain states allow you to argue the value of the tax deduction as a basis to reduce the support obligation. Review the appendix as to your applicable state law.

CHAPTER FOUR

Hearing Preparation

This is arguably the most important chapter of the book. The rest, almost without exception, deals with problems that begin here. A virtually endless amount of time and money can be saved through adequate preparation before any child support obligation is set.

Assuming that paternity is not in issue, an initial child support hearing is a little like an audit. In other words, the issue is decided based upon the numbers, with other factors having only a marginal effect.

Your primary task before the hearing is to have an accurate and organized presentation for the Court. A secondary task is to learn enough about the situation to present your case appropriately, In general, a sympathetic fact situation is of little use to a defendant who comes across as unsympathetic to the Court.

Although it can be difficult in these security conscious times, it is highly beneficial to go to the courthouse, and actually observe a few child support hearings before your court date. In most

57

jurisdictions, you should be able to gain entry once court security is satisfied that you pose no risk.

Essentially, this is an opportunity to study the judge and other court officials. . If possible, attempt to attend hearings with the same judge, and state attorney, as are involved in your own case. Try to attend an entire morning or afternoon session of Court.

Bring a notepad, listen and learn. Take careful notice of the arguments that are made, and how the Judge rules on each issue. Also, study whether the disposition of the Judge, and his or her rulings, change as the day wears on. Take careful note of whether the Judge gets listless or irritable near time for his mid-morning or lunch break.

If this is the case, do what you can to get heard early in the morning. Speak to the caseworker or the attorney for the social services agency, explain that you will be coming in early, and need to be out of the courthouse as soon as possible. If there is another legitimate reason for the request, such as a work commitment, mention this. It can make all the difference to have the ear of the Judge at a time when he or she will listen to you. .

Secondly, try to form an impression of the Judge's attitude towards the Defendants. As I have indicated repeatedly in this book, you will often find a strong bias towards the custodial parent. However, there can be differences among Judges, and these can be crucial.

For example, it is inevitable that some Defendants will argue for a downward deviation in their child support. Carefully document the response from the bench to each explanation, whether it is short term economic hardship, illness, unemployment or underemployment. Whether the Judge rules for the partcular Defendant is not as important, for your purposes as how receptive he or she appears to be towards the argument.

In other words, is the Judge attentively asking questions and evaluating exhibits, or does he simply shout down the protest of the Defendant? Does he or she show any signs of skepticism or irritation with the social workers or the attorney for the social services agency? If so, these are signs that the Court might be receptive to arguments related to your individual needs. In other words, the Court might cut you a break, and order you to pay less.

Also, take careful note of the surroundings. This would include how the defendants, and particularly the attorneys, are dressed, their language, and the kinds of exhibits they present to the Court. As much as possible, you will want to mimic the behavior of the most successful of these.

The purpose of this is twofold. Firstly, you will learn from the mistakes of the least successful litigants and their counsel. If a Judge seems particularly angered by an argument, you will know to avoid it. For example, I once represented a Defendant in a support case who had been fired because of an alcohol related traffic offense. The trial Judge has lost his son in an automobile accident caused by a drunk driver. This Judge was the worst possible audience for my client and his message.

Secondly, you will learn enough about the etiquette of the process to not stick out like a sore thumb. The more comfortable and competent you appear in the courtroom, the better you will be treated. Small details such as wearing a tie, and having multiple copies of exhibits, can make all the difference in your result. The best way to learn is first hand observation. This is particularly true because local standards vary so much.

In most jurisdictions, there are several Judges who might potentially hear your case. It is important to get an impression of the relative attitudes and tendencies of the group. While it is generally not possible to shop around for a Judge, as criminal defendants commonly do, the information is still useful.

For example, if you are scheduled before a Judge you particularly want to avoid, it might be possible to put off your hearing. This is called a continuance, and is normally granted due to illness, or some serious circumstance which makes a party to the action unavailable.

Otherwise, you will at least know what you are getting into. If you are satisfied, based on the best information, that you will be facing a "hanging judge", negotiating with the caseworker might suddenly be much more appealing.

As to these issues, it is always important to consider the source of the information. Keep in mind that when you ask a former litigant about a Judge, their opinion is neither objective nor detached. Many will see the facts of their situation in a highly partisan way, and consider themselves to have been treated unfairly, whether this is true or not.

If possible, try to get the opinions of attorneys, or persons who work in the courthouse. They can generally offer a more objective and informed opinion on the subject.

Do not ignore the possibility of finding help on the internet. In many areas, there are active support organizations for non-custodial fathers. A large group of sympathetic people with first hand experience can be a goldmine of information and support. There are similar organizations at many public assistance agencies and churches.

Once you have familiarized yourself with your audience, it is then necessary to take care in preparing your message. In the previous Chapter, we discussed the various methods by which child support is calculated. While there are important differences, they use much of the same information. As such, the first thing that must be considered is the issue of your own income and expenses.

62

There are a few situations which present obvious, recurring challenges. The first is the matter of employees or business owners whose income varies highly on a seasonal basis. There can be several reasons for this.

For example, I live in a resort area, which fills up with tourists during the summer months. I have many clients who make all of their money during the season, then take a winter siesta. Others are migrant farm workers, whose income is highly contingent on the weather.

The problem is, child support calculators presume a stable income, absent strong evidence to the contrary. If these facts are not properly presented, or interpreted in an unfair or lazy manner, serious consequences can occur.

There are several potential risks here. The first is that the caseworker simply takes the highest check stub, and calculates the support based upon the best month. The result is an unrealistically high child support calculation.

The second occurs if the father uses his lowest month. Since the state agency is likely to have a copy of his tax return, he runs of the risk of damaging his credibility with the Court. This can result in an unduly harsh order, due to a wrongful presumption that he lied about his income.

The safe course is to inform the caseworker and the Court that your income varies seasonally, and present evidence of your average income. The result will be a periodic support obligation that will be based upon your *average* income. As with every other expense, it will be imperative for an individual in this situation to save through the fat months to survive through the lean.

Another unique situation is the individual with a short term, or one time, cash windfall. This involves situations in which the Defendant has a large sum of money coming in such settlement proceeds from a lawsuit. In such cases, a great deal depends upon the characterization of the funds.

Often, monies received as compensation for permanent injury or disability, or for the compensation of medical expenses, will not be considered income for this purpose. Lost wages, on the other

64

hand, will be considered as income. There is the real possibility that a Court might order a portion of the lump sum proceeds paid over to the mother as an incident of support.

Another situation requiring special preparation and care is the one in which the

Defendant is either unemployed or underemployed. The term "underemployed" means that the father has a part time job, or is earning a wage far less than he might expect, considering his prior work history, education, and skills.

In such cases, the father runs the risk of a Judge determining that he is attempting to avoid paying support by refusing to work. In such cases, it is possible in virtually all jurisdictions to "attribute" what the Court considers a fair income to the non-custodial parent. When this happens, the plain message to the father is, get a full time job or an appropriate job, right now.

To rebut this argument, it is necessary to explain the why of the situation. If you are applying for work, bring copies of the cover letters and job applications, along with any responses you have

65

received. If you have suffered a work disruption due to a short term illness or injury, bring medical records; particularly, any evidence of temporary or permanent disability. Likewise, bring documentation of any disability insurance claim, workers compensation claim, or unemployment benefits claim.

At times, the task is simply to obtain proper evidence of income. Sometimes, a Federal W-2 or 1099 Form will suffice. More often, there is a required form or forms which must be submitted to the Court prior to the hearing.

Typically, the forms require disclosure of monthly income, payroll deductions, living expenses, and all assets such as cash on hand, or real property. The forms are required to be submitted under oath, like a tax return.

If you appear for Court unrepresented, you will ordinarily be handed such a form to fill out on the spot. Considering its importance, it is far wiser to obtain a copy in advance, and prepare it carefully. Decline the offer by a caseworker to take your check stubs or tax forms and fill the form out for you. This amounts to handing your case preparation over to the enemy.

You should be able to get a copy of the necessary form, either through the state child support agency website, or by contacting the agency directly. Get a copy well before the hearing, and study it carefully. Unless you prepare you own tax return, or have a high comfort level with math, consider getting help. The best sources would include your accountant, your attorney, or whoever else you might turn to when faced with complex financial issues.

The forms all follow a general format. The first, and most important thing, is to calculate income correctly. If you are a salaried employee, be sure to deduct everything withheld from you paycheck in calculating net income. This might seem obvious, but failure to do so is a frequent and costly mistake.

If your income is irregular for some reason, such as periodic bonuses or commissions, you will have to average your monthly income. This can be done by dividing your annual income by fifty two, then multiplying the total by four.

People tend to be lazy about estimating expenses, their own as well as those of the child. Take the time to go through personal checks or account records, so that these can be documented

67

accurately. Average out larger expenses that are paid infrequently, such as dental or medical bills.

The forms also require a statement as to assets in your possession, such as land, stock, or other investments. The Court will generally look at monthly income, and little else, in calculating the child support obligation. However, when there is a request for retroactive child support, or the father has insufficient income, this information might be crucial.

When these forms are filled out quickly, by persons under pressure, certain mistakes are common. The first, and arguably worst, relates to a personal residence or other real property owned by the father. Often, I have seen fathers simply list the property as an asset, at its full value.

The problem with this is one of perception. Although he occupies the house, if there is a mortgage, the reality is that he doesn't really own it. Rather, he ordinarily owns a small percentage in equity, and has the right to purchase the rest over a period of many years.

This leads to a misconception which I have sometimes seen corrected from the bench. I have seen a Judge review a financial declaration, look surprised, and ask the father if he owns his house outright. There would then be a discussion of the circumstances of the purchase, and an estimate of the equity in the home.

You cannot afford to assume that you will be so lucky. As such, it is important to do a little homework prior to the hearing.

You will have a mortgage interest statement attached to your tax return. It will show you, among other things, the balance due. If the statement is several months old, call the bank, and request updated figures from them. As in every case where information is important to your case, follow up your request in writing.

Next, you will need an estimated value for the property. The safest and often best value to use is the tax value. This can be found on your property tax receipt, or by contacting your local tax assessor. .

Once the figures are in hand, simply deduct the payoff on the mortgage from the tax value of the property. The resulting number is

69

the value of the property you will use on the financial declaration form.

For the same reason, you should check on the values of an investment or retirement accounts before filling out the form. This is usually a simple matter of either calling whatever party happens to manage the account. Again, it is essential to obtain written documentation to take to your hearing.

Keep in mind that it can take a substantial period of time to obtain some of this information. Banks tend to take several days to respond to account inquiries, at least in written form.

Health care providers, meanwhile, can be outright obstructionist when it comes to providing medical records or opinions. Unless you have a sympathetic doctor, your request for medical records will most likely be forwarded to a remote outpost in some foreign land. If you receive your records at all, the process will take months and substantial expense on your part.

In most states, there is also the possibility of a request for retroactive child support. This means that the mother is asking for back pay, from the time before the two of you went to court or earlier. Since several months can pass between the filing of the action and the hearing, the amount in issue can be substantial.

If you have been providing any kind of support to the child, bring receipts, records, and documentation. For this purpose, support can be defined as any benefit to the child, whether it is a weekly or bi-weekly cash payment, the purchase of necessities such as clothes, or simply keeping the child in your home.

I cannot emphasize enough that the financial issues here must be treated much like a tax audit. The father who does not get signed receipts for cash payments to the mother, or expenses paid on behalf of the child, is not thinking about litigation at the time. He is simply providing for his child, without any ulterior motive.

Too often, I have heard fathers complain after the hearing that the mother testified that they had done nothing for the child. Typically, the Judge will take the mother's story at face value, with the result being a substantial award of retroactive child support.

71

In some states, there are certain expenses that are immediately deducted from the child support obligation. The most common are medical or dental insurance for the child, and day care or school tuition. If these are being paid, check to see if the expense is deducted from the support obligation of the non-custodial parent in your state. Be sure to provide the Court with documentation of the fact that you pay these expenses.

The second part of the equation is the financial situation of the mother. In most cases, the father of the child will have relatively accurate information as to the mother's income. He will probably know if she works, and if so where. With that information, it is usually not difficult to verify income.

You will also receive a copy of her financial information prior to, or at, the hearing. It is still important to review it for accuracy. The most common area of abuse involves self employed mothers who work "under the table" for cash. Proving this can be a little like grabbing fog, without a witness who will testify in court as to her income.

The best way to do so is to show that the mother is living a life style beyond her means. For example, if the mother has an income near the poverty line, but owns a beach front condominium and a new car, a Judge might question the fairness of the situation. The same might occur if a current or former co-worker testified as to her "under the table" employment.

However, from the point of view of the mother, the worst inaccuracies are in the area of expenses. A common area of abuse is as to day care costs. Frequently, I have seen mothers pad the expense column with excessive payments to a relative or close friend who acts as the baby sitter. On a few occasion, the father has been able to actually prove that the expense was never paid, or was rebated.

This is particularly important if you state sets the child support payment based partially upon expenses incident to raising the child. If state procedural rules entitle you to early access to the mother's financial information, make every effort to get the records as soon as possible. This allows you to review the financial declaration well in advance, and attempt to verify any questionable expenses.

There is at least one essential tool available to you. In every state, you have a right to issue to issue a subpoena in a child support case. Before explaining how to use one, it first might be helpful to explain what a subpoena is.

A subpoena is, simply, a document issued by the Court, requiring a person to appear at a certain date and time. There is a specialized form of subpoena known as a "subpoena duces tecum", which requires a person or corporation to appear at a certain place or to produce certain things, such as documents or records.

The sad fact is, as you attempt to gather evidenced to help yourself, you will be met with indifference and hostility. Through the device of a subpoena, you can obtain the cooperation of persons and entities that would otherwise not help you.

For example, suppose that the mother is self employed, and you need to prove that her income is underreported. You might serve a subpoena on one of the companies with which she does business, requesting copies of the federal 1099 forms submitted to her at tax time. You night be able to seek out a disgruntled

74

employee, who could testify as to her habit of working for cash "under the table."

The same thing can be done as to the issue of expenses. If the private school tuition is shockingly high, you can subpoena the contract and payment records from the school. The same possibility exists as to other expenses such as day care costs.

The procedures for preparing and serving a subpoena vary somewhat from state to state. If you have an attorney, he or she will handle preparation and service.

However, it is essential that the two of you take time early on to discuss what documents or witnesses are needed at the hearing. There are time limits as to how much notice a party much be provided with to comply with a subpoena. If you wait too long, the court might refuse to enforce the subpoena if the witness refuses to comply.

If you are representing yourself, you will need to contact the County Clerk of Court. In my experience, the extent to which court officials cooperate with non-lawyers representing themselves varies

75

tremendously from jurisdiction to jurisdiction. Explain your situation, and request that you be provided the number of subpoenas you need.

There are options if you meet with resistance. In the case of an outright refusal, write a certified letter to the office of the Clerk of Court, documenting his or her non-cooperation. Insist that a copy of the letter be placed in your file, and explain why the evidence sought through the subpoena is necessary to your case.

You can also insist that the Clerk schedule a hearing before the trial judge to resolve the issue. Often, this tactic will get you what you need, thought it won't make you any friends in the courthouse.

Each subpoena has to be served on each defendant. The states uniformly prohibit the service of such documents by a party to the action. This mean that you cannot simply go find the party in question, and hand a copy to him or her.

Instead, you will have to either hire a private detective to serve the subpoena, or have it served through local law enforcement. As you might expect, the private detective is the more expensive option. For the price, however, you can expect the job to be handled with more urgency, and attentiveness to your needs.

The choice should be based upon the time considerations involved, as well as your level of trust with local law enforcement. The closer you are to a hearing date, the more it makes sense to take on the cost of a private process server.

There are other costs related to serving a subpoena on a party. There is always a standard appearance fee due and owing to the party who is required to appear. In most states, this amount is nominal.

However, the expenses can be substantially higher when the witness is required to locate or reproduce records, especially medical records. Health care providers often charge several dollars a page for notes, charts, and even bills. Anticipate writing a substantial check if you obtain compliance at all.

If you seek medical records for the mother or the child, you will probably require consent from the mother. There is a standard form called a "Medical Authorization", which must be executed and presented to the health care provider in order to obtain the records.

You would make your request to the state support agency, the private attorney representing the mother, or the unrepresented mother. When the form is properly executed, the health care provider will have no choice but to provide the records you request.

If your request is refused, your option is to schedule a hearing. You would explain to the Judge what records you are seeking, and why they are important to your case. If you are persuasive, the Court has the authority to make the mother and her lawyer cooperate and sign the medical authorization. .

I have included a standard Federal District Court subpoena in the appendix. This is not the exact form you will be using. The litigation of child support matters is exclusively within the jurisdiction of state courts. However, the language and content varies little from one jurisdiction to another, so the federal form is highly instructive.

What is essential to understand is the nature of the document. Rather than a request for information by you, it is an order issued by the court. If the individual fails to appear, or to produce the requested documents, he or she runs the risk of being held in contempt of court.

By serving a subpoena, you invoke the authority of the Court in helping you prove your case. There is no more powerful discovery tool.

No later than a week prior to the hearing, you should organize you materials you will need. Do this early, while you still have time to make engage in additional investigation, or address any problems with your file.

The following items should always be included. Remember that, if a document is to be presented as evidence to the Court, you can expect to need three copies, one for the Court, one for your file, and one for the opposing party.

1. Your financial disclosure form.
2. Copies of any subpoenas served
3. Copies of proof of service of subpoenas from sheriff or process server

79

4. All documents produced in response to subpoenas

5. Financial disclosure form of the mother

6. The petition for child support relief initially served on you

7. Any responsive pleading filed by you

CHAPTER FIVE

The Hearing

The child support obligation is usually set through a two step process. Initially, there is an administrative hearing. This is a meeting between you, a state employee, and possibly the custodial parent.

The purpose of the administrative hearing is to resolve the contested issues, if at all possible. Ideally, this would include paternity and child support. If not, it is still an opportunity to collect and exchange information prior to a judicial hearing.

Expect to wait a long time before the hearing. When you arrive, you will be ushered into a crowded waiting room, full of non-custodial parents, custodial parents, and a surprising number of children.

The social services agencies usually set dozens of hearings in a single day. The best chance to move to the front of the line is to arrive early. This is particularly true if you do not have an attorney. Be sure to notify the court of your presence when you arrive, and

81

confirm that you are in the right place. Even if you rely on a written notice, it is possible that the hearing has been moved or postponed.

Usually, the first person you will deal with directly is the caseworker. This individual might or might not be an attorney, but will invariably be an employee of the state agency which prosecutes support cases. It is crucial to understand their role in the process.

The caseworker is a trained product of the state social services system. As such, he or she has been trained, and approved for hire, by the same people who coined the phrase "dead beat dad." Every day, this person works in an office surrounded by posters depicting "Most Wanted" non-custodial parents, usually with six figure arrearages and pending warrants.

His or her first objective is to get you to acknowledge paternity, if you have not done so already. The second is to get you to agree to pay child support based upon the state guidelines.

There is nothing dishonest or unethical about this. However, it is important to understand that the case worker is in no way a mediator, seeking a middle ground between your interest and that of the custodial parent. Rather, he or she is a hired gun who represents two interests, that of the state support agency, and of the custodial parent.

The problem is one of perception. To most defendants, the case worker has the appearance of a court official. He or she may have an office set up right on the premises, is a government employee, and has decision making authority. Too often, the non-custodial parent simply hands his pay stub over to the caseworker, and waits submissively to be told how much to pay.

In other comparable situations, the law sets forth extensive protections for unrepresented parties. Without exception, every state code of attorney ethics has detailed regulations designed to prevent lawyers from bullying or tricking unrepresented parties.

However, in child support cases, I regularly see tactics which would be problematic for a door to door salesman. Too often, the non-custodial parent is simply unaware that he has options and rights.

So how should a defendant deal with a caseworker? Essentially, the same way you would with a car salesman. The analogy might seem harsh, but it underscores the point perfectly.

If you were going to a dealership to buy a new car, you would come prepared. You would be aware, for example, that the sticker price of the car is almost always negotiable. For this reason, you would have taken the time to research the price of the vehicle.

You would know that the salesman works on commission, and has an incentive to sell the car at the highest possible price. You would also be aware that the salesman has limited negotiating authority, and that somebody else will probably broker and approve the deal. With this information, you are in a position to negotiate confidently. In a child support case, this would mean that you:

- Havre accurate knowledge and documentation of your income for the full year.

- Have accurate knowledge and documentation of the income of the custodial parent's income for the full year

- Have accurate knowledge and documentation of any child related expense used in calculating the support obligation in your state

- Have receipts and records for all expenses you have paid on behalf of the child which were not Court ordered.

- Have a preliminary calculation of child support.

- If you are unemployed or underemployed, have documentation of the reasons for this, and of your attempts to obtain full time employment.

Before you agree to any order establishing paternity, always insist on a paternity test. Remember, you have an absolute constitutional right to the test. However, a waiver of this right is often irrevocable, regardless of the circumstances. There is simply too much at stake, on too many levels, to acknowledge paternity without proof.

I know of no other situation in which a category of defendants is urged to waive a constitutional right, without adequate counsel. If the same individuals were charged with misdemeanor traffic violations, they would be given extensive, cautionary advice.

For example, a defendant would be told of his right to a trial by jury, to confront witnesses, and to cross examination. He would be required to knowingly waive each right in order to plead guilty to the charge. If he expressed any doubt as to what he was doing, the court would be unwilling to accept his guilty plea.

Yet, the typical child support defendant is encouraged to waive his constitutional right to paternity testing, and his refusal to do so is met with barely concealed hostility. It is a stated goal of the Federal government to encourage men to voluntarily acknowledge paternity, by the execution of a form affidavit.

This is in spite of the fact much of his income, and ultimately in many cases, his freedom is at issue. As such, if paternity has not been determined scientifically, insist on this. The Judge will be aware that you have an absolute right to a paternity test, even if you are unable to pay for it. There is no need to negotiate further until the test results prove you are the father.

If that issue is resolved, at least explore the possibility of settling the case through negotiation. Notwithstanding my concerns expressed earlier, it is possible that the case worker has an open and fair mind.

For example, several years ago, I filed a petition to reduce child support for a client. His problem was underemployment. He worked in a depressed industry, and his hours had been dramatically reduced. This made it impossible for him to continue paying a support obligation which had been set in the best earning year of his life.

Unfortunately, the two mothers of his three children were unsympathetic. He was also dealing with a federal tax lien which was siphoning off what little remained of his paycheck. He was behind on the support obligation, living off the good will of relatives, and in constant feat of arrest.

To her credit, the case worker reviewed the financial records in the file, and conceded my point. She agreed to a modification of the two support orders, more in line with the drastic decrease in his income. Unfortunately, the two mothers refused to sign off on the settlement. After a two hour hearing, the Judge asked my client if he was in good health, and advised him to get a second job. The support obligation remained unchanged.

If you are able to reach an agreement, be careful to note the date for the first payment. Expect the payments to start almost immediately. If your hearing is set on any day other than Friday, the initial payment will ordinarily be due on the Friday of the week of the hearing.

It is important that the Order specify the method by which the initial payment will be made. There can be a substantial delay between the date of the hearing, and the filing of the order. Until then, the Court system will be unable to receive and disburse your payment.

The risk is that payments made by you, or wages withheld and forwarded by your employer, will not be properly received or documented. Such a misunderstanding could make it appear that you are in contempt of Court, and lead to an unnecessary, stressful, and expensive hearing. This problem can be solved in advance, by addressing the issue in the support order.

88

If you are unable to agree to the amount of support, your case will be brought before a Judge. Unfortunately, there is no constitutional guarantee to a jury trial in a child support case. As such, a family court Judge will have decision making authority over your case.

In discussing Judges, many of the same considerations apply as with caseworkers. There is, however, one crucial difference. In this case, the appearance of state power and decision making authority is real.

You are stuck with the Judge as a fact finder and decision maker, absent a miracle such as postponement due to illness or other emergency.

Since you lack choice in the matter, you simply have to make the best o things. There is also good news, Most Judges pride themselves in their autonomy, and to some extent will listen to your side of the case. In my experience, some even become disillusioned with the state agencies over time, and are actually receptive to the arguments of non-custodial parents.

Nevertheless, the reality is that you face an uphill battle in court. Too often, I have been in chambers with a family court Judge on a morning when he or she is faced with multiple child support contempt hearings, and heard a comment such as "Well, let's go throw some men in jail."

The obvious conclusion is that his or her mind is already made up. At the very least, such comments suggest a troubling bias. It can be a huge challenge to convince the Judge that the hearing is more than a formality, and that your side of the story is worth listening to.

Of course, I practice in the state of South Carolina. This is a traditionally Republican, conservative state, with a skeptical attitude towards big government and social programs. It would be reasonable to expect that my state would be more sympathetic than most to the non-custodial parent. My educated guess is that, elsewhere, things are worse.

Since, at this point, we are discussing the initial child support hearing, you can anticipate less negativity than a defendant in a contempt action. The key is to avoid actions or representations

90

which will allow the Judge, in his or her mind, to categorize you as a "dead beat dad", shout down your argument, and go hurriedly to the next case.

The first considerations are obvious. For example, most Judges place great importance on appearance. As such, it is important to look and act the part of someone respectful of the Court as an institution.

This means, as much as possible, dressing the part. So break out your one suit that fits, put on a tie, and go conservative. I once saw a circuit court Judge in a small town give a lawyer thirty minutes to get a haircut and be back in the courtroom, or be held in contempt. Times have changed, but remember, to many older Judges still on the bench, those were the good old days.

Avoid the stupid mistakes that sour a Judge immediately and irrevocably. For example, most courtrooms have signs that read "No Cell Phones." I can tell you that they mean business. To avoid even the slightest risk of a ringing cell phone, many attorneys just leave them in the car.

Avoid interrupting or talking out of turn. Even the most patient of Judges will quickly lose his or her temper with a disruptive party. You will inevitably get your turn to speak. If you attempt to disrupt, distract, or intimidate the opposing party, you waste the opportunity by destroying your credibility.

Be ready when you are called to appear. This might mean bringing a buddy along to cover you during bathroom or smoke breaks. If your name is called, and you fail to appear, several bad things can happen. The worst is the possibility of the Court holding you in default, and giving the custodial parent or the state whatever they want.

Alternately, the Court might simply call the next case, move you to the back of the line, and let you wait a (long) while longer. When your name is finally called again, you can safely assume that the Judge will be tired and irritable, and will remember you as "the guy who didn't hear his name."

When you enter the courtroom, look to the bailiff for directions. The bailiff is a court official who, among other things, handles security for the Judge. He or she will direct you to a seat, usually

92

a table. The opposing party will be seated at a table opposite you.

First, take a few moments to organize your exhibits for the hearing. There should be three or four copies of each item, one for you, the Judge, and each opposing party. Place the exhibits from left to right, in the order in which you plan to use them.

Since you are the Defendant, you will ordinarily not have the opportunity to speak first. Listen carefully to the testimony presented by the opposing party, and take notes. You might need to object to testimony or documents presented at this stage, as described later in this book.

If the custodial parent testifies, you will have the opportunity to cross examine her. Unless you are contesting the issue of paternity, you should carefully limit the nature of the questions. These are the important objectives of a cross examination of the mother:

- Verify income of the mother from all sources
- Verify amount of her declared child related expenses

- Challenge any expenses that are suspiciously high

- Verify any cash or non-cash benefits you have provided for the child

- Verify any extended visitation above and beyond alternating weekends

- Verify through the mother that you are a concerned and caring father.

The goal here is to turn the tables, by having the opposing party confirm all, or party of the story. To a trial lawyer, the process of cross examination is an art. It is also the time honored method for arriving at truth in a court of law.

This is due to the unique nature of the process. When a witness takes the stand, he or she can expect to be questioned on behalf of each party. The process begins with the direct examination, which is conducted by the "friendly" party. The questions will be intended to elicit testimony which is usually rehearsed, and favorable to the party who brought the witness to Court.

After the direct testimony, the opposing party has the opportunity to cross examine the witness. Unlike direct examination,

94

cross examination is intended to discredit either the witness or the factual basis of the testimony.

The witness can hardly be expected to cooperate in this. If the opposing party were limited to asking conventional, open ended questions, the process of cross examination would be futile. However, the process of cross examination is a powerful tool in skilled hands. This is because the opposing party is allowed to ask leading questions.

So what is a leading question? A leading question is a question which suggests the answer. For example:

- You received two hundred dollars in cash from me last week, didn't you?

- I have kept the medical insurance premiums current, haven't I?

- These receipts are for items I bought for the child with my own money aren't they?

95

Once you have familiarized yourself with the form, you should have no trouble preparing to cross examine a witness. Take the time to write out the questions well before the hearing.

You can interrupt a witness who wants to explain her answer beyond the simple yes or no response. Be polite but aggressive about doing so. Interrupt by saying, "I simply need you to answer yes or no."

A well planned cross examination will build your case before you ever take the stand. At the least, the mother might be forced to back off unfair, hard words. At best, you might have the opportunity to destroy her credibility and with it her testimony.

It is possible to win a case outright during cross examination. Several years ago, I tried a case in which paternity was an issue. The father had consented to an adjudication of paternity, a crucial error. He later obtained information which led him to believe he was not the father of the child. The mother did not want the court to order a blood test.

During direct examination, the mother testified that her only sexual partner during the possible period of conception was her husband. It happened that she had separated from him about ten months prior to the birth.

I had been provided medical records from her gynecologist, which told a different story. The records were from about two and a half weeks later. The nurse had helpfully noted that the patient indicated having had sexual intercourse "several times in the past week."

Given that information, the rest was essentially shooting fish in a barrel. First, I asked her to confirm a few specific dates:

Q: So you separated from your husband on September 1, 2000?

A: Yes.

Q: That is the exact date on which you separated, isn't it?

A? Yes.

97

Q: And you filed a Complaint for divorce the next day, didn't you?

A: Yes.

Q: And you never had sexual intercourse with your husband after that date, did you?

A: No.

Q: I am handing you a document. This is a record of your visit to your gynecologist on September 21, 2000, isn't it?

A: Yes.

Q: And you told the nurse that you had sexual intercourse several times during that week, didn't you?

A: (After a long silence) She's a lair.

My client got his paternity test, which proved that he was not the father of the child. It turned out that the mother had been living with the actual father for a few months. The relationship then soured. She now collects support from the man who should rightfully be paying it.

There would ordinarily be no witness other than the custodial parent. You will then be given the opportunity to speak. The Judge will often seem restless by the time your turn comes around, which is understandable considering the number of hearings that are packed into the allotted time. Keep your cool, and resist the pressure to surrender the floor prematurely.

That being said, you do not benefit by wasting the court's time. In fact, there are several sure loser arguments that you should avoid *entirely*. Resist any urge to go in any of these directions.

> 1. **Attack the mother. Unless** the Court is also going to rule on the issue of custody, and there is a legitimate issue as to the fitness of the mother, avoid personal attacks.

For some people, this is an almost irresistible impulse. This is certainly understandable. There's sure to be plenty of hostility in the room considering the circumstances.

Still, you must resist the urge to tell the mother what you think of her at the worst possible time. You lose points with the Judge for several reasons.

ROBERT W. RUSHING JR.

First of all, it has nothing to do with the issue to be decided by the Court. There are few better ways to annoy most Judges than to waste Court time.

Secondly, it plays badly with the initial prejudices of most Judges. Rightly or not, the mother is considered a hero of sorts. After all, she is the one raising the child; presumably with little assistance from you.

The Judge is likely to take any attack on the character of the mother as proof of your "dead beat" behavior," and bad character.

> **2. Attack the Child.** The same considerations apply here, except even moreso. Attacking the mother is at least justifiable in situations of abuse or neglect, or to a lesser extent, when the father is a highly involved parent. Directing the personal attack at the child is a true "no-win" situation.

This is because whatever failings you attribute to the child will inevitably are blamed upon you. If the child has no interest in seeing you or talking to you, this is presumably because of parental

100

Copyright © 2010 Robert W. Rushing, Jr. All rights reserved.

neglect. If the child is disrespectful, this is the logical result of your absence from the home.

Any argument along these grounds is sure to backfire.

3. Attempt to use Visitation Issues as a Shield against the Child Support Obligation. The fact is, you do have a right to access to your child. In most places, the Courts will enforce the visitation rights of the non-custodial parent with at least luke-warm enthusiasm.

However, the obligation to pay child support is not conditioned upon access to the child. When I talk to fathers who are behind on child support, this is the first explanation I hear. Unfortunately, it is an argument that always lands on the courtroom floor with a dull thud.

Even if you are sincere about wanting to see your child, the court will not use the child support obligation as "bait" to force cooperation from the mother.

You can expect a standard response to this argument. 'You need to file a petition with the court seeking visitation. We will

101

address your issue at that time. The exception, of course, is in the few states that do address visitation issues at a hearing to establish child support.

4. Argue that the expenses of a new wife and step children as a basis to reduce the obligation. As far as the court is concerned, when you take on new dependants, you do so fully aware of your responsibility for old ones. For this reason, the financial consequences of a remarriage are not likely to gain you relief or sympathy. This is particularly true because you have no legal obligation to support step children, unless you have adopted them.

5. Argue that "new dad" should support the child. The logical flip side of this argument involves the situation where the mother is cohabiting with another man. Often, the mother actually encourages the replacement of the father of the children by "new-dad" as a source of emotional, if not financial, support. It would seem logical that, at least in some cases, this would be a relevant topic in a support action.

It is not. To understand why, it is necessary to understand the primary objective of the state in a support action. The objective is to find a person who can be legally bound to support the child through court order. This benefits the state by 1) avoiding the necessity of the state supporting the child through welfare agencies, and 2) providing a secondary source of support, should the custodial parent become unable or unwilling to support the child.

Simply put, the "new-dad" cannot fit the bill. He has no obligation to support the children, even if he marries the mother. The only way he will have such an obligation is if an adoption occurs. The state is looking for someone to make payments and guarantee the expenses of the child, like a bank seeking a co-signor for a loan. The natural father is the only real candidate.

6. Argue for a downward deviation from the support guidelines based upon losing a job, or taking a lower paying job, by choice. The courts are particularly attuned to the idea that a non-custodial parent might manipulate his income in anticipation of a child support hearing. While this does occur, my own belief is that the scenario is more urban myth than reality.

Unless the non-custodial parent is self employed, or has an employer willing to conspire with him to deceive the court, this "strategy" inevitably does more harm to the non-custodial parent than the custodial parent.

Unlike the others, this is an argument you might have to make where the circumstances exist. If so, prepare for an uphill battle in justifying your decision.

7. Argue for a downward deviation from the support guidelines based upon expenses that can be considered luxurious or lavish. This is only common sense. Still, I have actually seen non-custodial parents argue that the expenses of maintaining horses, hobby cars, or a jet ski is a legitimate basis for reducing the support payment.

When you attempt this, you look like Wile E. Coyote running towards the cliff. Besides the fact that the argument is a loser, it further damages your case by reminding the Court that you have expendable income, and mistaken priorities.

8. Argue that personal gifts to the child amount to child support. This is not an absolute rule. However, be careful in arguing that gifts to the child are a form of support. This is especially true if the gifts are given for an occasion, such as a holiday.

It might be appropriate to make this argument if the "gift" was substantial in value, and a benefit to the health, education, or development of the child. In other words, to provide school clothes, books, or a computer, would arguably be considered support. A video game or a skate board would almost certainly not be.

9. Argue that the system is unfair. The child support system is what it is. This book has a great deal to say about what is wrong with the process.

Nevertheless, even the most benign Judge is sworn to uphold the law as it exists in the books. The best response you can expect to your fairness argument is "That's an issue to take up with the politicians." At worst, you are baiting the wolf by asking his help in guarding your chickens.

10. Attacking the Court. If you want to insure that bad things happen, not only at the first hearing, but at future hearings, attack the Court. The Judge will hand opposing counsel a blank check with your name on it, and fill in any amount.

Worse, you will be remembered and punished again at your next hearing. Hold your tongue and engage in some primal scream therapy after the fact. I have never heard of a kamikaze attack that worked out well for the kamikaze.

So what should you present at the hearing? You should open by raising any issues that might prevent the Court from ordering you to pay child support. These would include:

- Paternity is disputed.
- You are disabled.
- You have legal or physical custody of the child.
- You are in the United States military at a time of war.

The first several of these need no elaboration. Again, if you dispute paternity, insist on a paternity test. You have a right to the test, even if you cannot afford to pay for it.

If you are disabled, bring medical proof to the hearing. If you have legal custody of the child, bring a copy of the court order with you. After the order is admitted into evidence, the situation will take care of itself.

If you are exercising physical custody of the child without the authority of a court order, the situation is more problematic. This occurs frequently when the mother relocates, simply leaving the child with the father.

Frequently, the state agency is not aware of the change in the situation. It therefore acts to enforce the order after the father stops paying. I have often seen the mother leave the child with the father, and relocate to pursue a new relationship, still intending to enforce the support obligation.

The justifications can vary. I have heard mothers explain that the continued support is compensation for all her years of hard work. This, of course, does not take into account that the child, who is now living with the father, is being effectively deprived of financial support.

I have also heard mothers claim that the relocation of the child is an "extended visitation" for the father. Presumably, the mother intends to reclaim the child later, when she is confident in her new job or relationship. If this arrangement extends for more than a few weeks, it is unfair not to make at least some financial adjustment on behalf of the father and child.

Ideally, you would have a hearing to approve the change in custody. However, often the mother absolutely will not cooperate in this. The father must choose between taking the child without court approval, and losing him or her.

In such a case, attempt to get some form of written documentation from the mother. If this is only a hand written note, or an e-mail, it is still better than nothing.

While neither of these is nearly as good as a court order, they do provide certain advantages. They are typically admissible in court, and can prove that the mother acted voluntarily. This can be crucial.

You must also keep careful records of your own. Maintain a calendar from the date the child was relocated to your home, recording each day that the child resides with you. It might also be helpful to present independent witnesses as to the situation. For example, neighbors, relatives, teachers, or friends can reliably testify to the fact that the child resides in your home.

If you are an active member of the United States military, you are subject to the provisions of the Soldier's and Sailor's Relief Act. It shields you from all court proceedings during time of war, provided you are in deployment. This is an issue which, ideally, would be raised well prior to the date of the hearing.

The remaining issues to be presented here have been discussed in Chapters Three and Four. To repeat, they are as follows:

1. Present accurate documentation of your own income.

2. Explain any seasonal or commission based fluctuation in income.

3. Address any overtime situation, and whether it is subject to change in the future.

4. Present proof of any tax liens.

5. Present copies of any other child support orders to which you are subject.

6. Present proof of any major and necessary personal expense.

7. Present proof of any inconsistencies as to mother's financial disclosure.

8. Present proof of any inconsistencies or exaggerations as to mother's declared expenses.

9. Present proof of day care, medical, or dental expenses paid on behalf of the child.

This list includes all of the necessary information to allow for the fair calculation of child support. Provided that all applicable figures are considered, the court should arrive at a figure you can live with.

It is essential to be sure that every item of income or expense used to calculate child support is fair and accurate. Remember, small mistakes, multiplied over months and years, can amount to thousands of dollars in overpayments.

CHAPTER SIX

Basic Evidence Law

Before your hearing, you should know some things about evidence law. It might be possible that no issue as to admissibility of evidence arises. However, if it does, failure to have at least a general knowledge of this area of the law could be bad for your financial health.

The key is to know when to object. This is because, as to the defendant, you will not speak first, nor present much of the evidence. Instead, the attorney for the custodial parent, or the state support agency, will present the majority of the case.

111

In rapid succession, the evidence as to issues such as paternity, income of the custodial parent, expenses of the custodial parent, as well as your own income and expenses, will be presented. If you fail to object, the testimony and physical exhibits are entered into evidence, and the basis for the support order.

By your silence, you allow inadmissible evidence to enter the record as fact. In this manner, you might easily lose your case before even opening your mouth. So, what kind of evidence is admissible under the rules of evidence? Although there are some differences among state laws, the principles are surprisingly consistent.

The best way to explain how the process works is by explaining the *reasons* why certain evidence is not admissible.

Hearsay: The most common objection to testimony offered by the Court, or certain content of documents, is that the material is hearsay. There are countless legal definitions of the term, but the concept is fairly simple. Basically, you cannot repeat in Court what another person said to you who is *not* in Court, to prove the truth of what was said.

112

There is an obvious, common sense reason for this. Since the person who actually said the thing is not around, he or she cannot be cross examined. The Court cannot evaluate the reliability of the words, by learning more about the person who said them and the circumstances.

For example, you might be seeking a Court order for a paternity test. The mother of the child takes the stand, and says, "Everybody knows that's his kid. His father was telling everyone how proud he was and handing out cigars."

Is this admissible testimony? Actually, that would depend on whether the father she refers to is you, or your own father.

If the words are attributed to you, they are admissible. This is because you are present in Court, with the opportunity to deny or explain the statement. For this reason, it is possible to evaluate the reliability of the testimony.

On the other hand, if the statement is attributed to the *grandfather* of the child, it is inadmissible. Since he is presumably not in Court, it is impossible to evaluate the reliability of the testimony through cross examination.

The next question is whether the testimony is offered to prove the truth of the statement. In this case, it certainly is. The mother wants to prove that you, the putative father, acknowledged paternity. She has a definite interest in the outcome, and the accuracy of her representation is open to question. The testimony is inadmissible.

In general, stand up and be ready to object when you hear such phrases as "He said…," "She told me…," "The medical records said," or "A lot of people know that…"

At this point, you would object. You do this by simply saying "I object." Unlike other situations, in this case, it is appropriate to interrupt the witness on the stand or the opposing lawyer.

The Judge will ask you to state the grounds for the objection. You would indicate that the testimony is inadmissible hearsay. The Judge will rule as to whether the testimony will be allowed into evidence. The case will then proceed.

There is another way that lawyers get hearsay evidence admitted into a case. This usually involves documents, such as medical or financial records. They often simply hand documents up to the Judge, without providing a copy to the opposing party. They then ask that the documents be admitted into evidence.

The Judge will then ask the opposing party if he has any objection. Most people interpret the question as a request. In accordance with the perceived wish of the authority figure, they say no.

This is a HUGE mistake. For the same reason you would never allow the custodial parent to hand notes up to the Judge, you cannot allow documents to be entered into evidence that you have not reviewed. This can be the legal equivalent of a sword to the stomach, depending on the contents of the documents.

Instead, ALWAYS ask the Court for a copy of the document, and time to review it carefully.

At this point, you cannot allow yourself to be pressured. There is a reasonable possibility that somebody is trying to pull a fast one on you. While probably not a smoking gun, it is safe to assume that something in the document is harmful to you.

There are a lot of exceptions to the hearsay rule. The Federal Rules of evidence list twenty four: Those relevant for our purposes include the following:

1. Business records, including those of a public agency;

2. Evidence of the absence of a business records or entry;

3. Certain public records or reports;

4. Records of vital statistics;

5. Marriage, baptism, or similar certificates;

6. Records of religious organizations concerning family history.

These documents are considered inherently reliable, and might well be admitted into evidence despite the hearsay objection. However, there is still the possibility that there is hearsay within the document.

In other words, a document might be admissible for a purpose. However, certain information contained in it might not be admissible.

116

A medical record that details prescribed medications is admissible for that purpose. However, the handwritten notes of the nurse, noting that "child's father is listed incorrectly on the birth certificate," would not be.

This is the reason why such documentation must be carefully reviewed. If you object, such damaging comments can be deleted from the record, and from consideration in the case.

The second large category of exceptions to the hearsay rule involves testimony used to attack the credibility of a witness. It makes perfect sense that a person who has told different versions of a story at different times be held accountable.

There are exceptions to the hearsay rule which provide for this. Prior statements by a witness that are inconsistent with his or her present testimony, and that were made under oath, are admissible. Likewise, prior statements by a witness that are consistent with his or her present testimony, when offered to rebut a charge of fabrication, are admissible. In general, there is a good chance that the prior statements of a witness will be admitted into evidence by a court.

117

Copyright © 2010 Robert W. Rushing, Jr. All rights reserved.

Statements of this nature are considered by the federal rules to be non-hearsay. They are freely admissible for every use at trial. In some states, all prior inconsistent statements of a witness are admissible (See California Rules of Evidence, Code Section 769, 1235.)

The final category of exceptions to the hearsay rule involves statements made under circumstances which would tend to make them reliable. These things are said with an urgent need to communicate accurately, or without incentive or motivation to lie.

These include:

1. Statements against interest.
2. Reputation of a person's character.
3. Excited utterances.
4. Statements made for the purposes of medical diagnosis or treatment.
5. Dying declarations.

It is beyond the scope of this book to engage in an extended discussion of the hearsay rule. The best approach for a defendant is to raise the hearsay objection where he sees it. After the basis for the objection is stated, it is up to the other side to argue the exception.

Evidence which is not hearsay still might not be admissible. Even the most complex of trials is calculated to resolve a particular dispute between parties. To avoid the confusion and save time, there are constraints on who can testify, and about what.

The rules in this area are tied to the rules of pleading. When you are served with papers, they serve as notice of what the opposing party wants from you. Your trial preparation is based upon the idea of responding to the content of the papers. For this reason, the opposing party is limited in what he or she can present as testimony.

For example, suppose you are sued for damages due to an automobile accident. The person you hit is also your next door neighbor. While he is testifying about how you backing into his parked car, he recalls something else.

"By the way," he says, "I also want him to return my lawn mower and pay me fair rental value. He's kept the thing for over a year now, and won't return it."

Without knowing a thing about evidence law, you know that he cannot do this. The case is about the automobile accident, not anything else. I use this concept to introduce several concepts as to the admissibility of evidence.

In general, Evidence must be relevant, material, and competent to be admissible. If so, it is admissible, unless a specific exclusionary rule applies.

Evidence is *relevant* when it has any tendency in reason to make the fact that it is offered to prove or disprove either more or less probable (Federal Rules of Evidence Rule 401). To be relevant, the item of evidence does not have to prove the fact for which it is offered. In fact, it does not even have to make the fact more probable than not. However, the item of evidence must have some tendency to increase the likelihood of the fact for which it is offered.

Evidence is *material* if it is offered to prove a fact that is at issue in the case. Evidence which is relevant to prove a certain fact would still be inadmissible if it is immaterial.

For example, suppose you are involved in a child support case. The mother of the child produces her credit card and records to prove that she made payments on an engagement ring. The evidence might be relevant to prove that she made payments on the ring. However, unless she has requested reimbursement for the payments in her pleadings, the evidence is immaterial. It is therefore not admissible.

Evidence is *competent* if the proof that is being offered meets certain traditional requirements of reliability. The preliminary showing that the evidence meets those tests, and any other prerequisites of admissibility, is called *foundation* evidence. When an objection is made that an answer to a question, a document, or a thing lacks a proper foundation, the basis for the objection is that competence or some other prerequisite of admissibility has not been shown.

For example, there are certain requirements that are the foundation for competent witness testimony. They are as follows:

1. The witness must, with understanding, take the oath or a substitute.

2. The witness must have personal knowledge about the subject of the testimony.

3. The witness must remember what he saw, heard, or perceived.

4. The witness must be able to communicate what he perceived.

Similarly, most documents offered into evidence will have to be authenticated. By this process, testimony is offered to demonstrate in what manner the document was obtained, handled, and preserved prior to trial. The purpose is to prove that the item authentically is what it is supposed to be, and has not been tampered with.

The common scenario in which the issue would arise in a support action involves the paternity test. As we discussed earlier, there is the possibility that human error or fraud could alter the results of such a test. For this reason, the defendant might want to question the technician who performed the test.

If a paternity test has determined that you are the father of a child, your entire case rests on the success of this argument. It is then essential to show that court that, contrary to popular misconception, the tests are subject to a high probability of human error.

This is a highly technical argument, which should ideally be presented by an attorney. In support of this position, it might well be necessary to retain a medical expert. Certainly, the amount of money at stake will frequently justify such an expense.

Typically, a Judge will seriously consider an objection to the relevance of evidence. This is because all Courts operate under severe time constraints. As such, they must collect information in the most efficient manner possible. They cannot do so when witnesses get off the subject, and testify to matter which has nothing to do with the issue to be resolved.

For the same reason, a Judge will carefully evaluate an objection to the materiality of testimony or evidence. However, immaterial evidence is presented at trial with much less frequency than irrelevant evidence.

Attorneys and witnesses offer inadmissible evidence for two primary reasons. The first is to portray a witness in a bad light, by providing negative evidence as to his or her character. The hope is to thereby prejudice the Court against the litigant.

The second is based upon a misunderstanding of the rules of evidence. A witness who is either unrepresented, or poorly prepared, will often testify in a rambling, disorganized fashion. Without a proper direct examination, the witness will continue to wander further and further off the subject. In both cases, the result is irrelevant testimony.

By contrast, the category of immaterial evidence is just a smaller sub-group. The evidence in question is directed towards a subject relevant to the Court. The problem is that the testimony or exhibit in question serves no purpose for interpreting the facts.

For example, suppose you were a defendant in a paternity case. You testified that you were in another state on the day that the child was allegedly conceived. Your testimony is relevant to the issue of whether you are the father of the child. However, you could still provide evidence that is immaterial.

For example:

"I was in Nevada that day. I bought three sweatshirts at Wal-Mart. They were on sale. I remember I paid twenty eight dollars for the sweat shirts. They were brown."

The fact that you were in Nevada is relevant. The fact that you went to a Wal-Mart there and bought the sweat shirts is material, because it tends to prove out the fact that you were in Nevada. (If you were the defendant in this case, note how much you could help yourself by producing a receipt or credit card record of the purchase. This would be strong proof that you were in Nevada at the time of conception, and could possibly win the case for you.)

However, the fact that the sweatshirts were brown is immaterial. That fact does nothing to prove or disprove that you

125

were in Nevada on that date. For the same reason, the price of the sweatshirt is immaterial. This testimony would be excluded if objected to.

It is also possible to object to the foundation of evidence. This occurs frequently when the evidence in question is a physical exhibit such as a medical record. By objecting, you demand proof of where the evidence came from, and how it has been maintained, preserved, and stored. This is called the "chain of custody."

In many cases, the rules of evidence require little or no proof of "chain of custody." This is because of the considerable time and expense that can be involved. Even when the objection is appropriate, the Court will strictly limit the extent of testimony as to this issue.

However, if the evidence is crucial to the case, the objection should be raised. This is especially true in the case of technical evidence, dispositive to the issue in the case, in which the individual who performed the procedure will not otherwise appear.

When the objection if raised, there are two possible outcomes. The Judge could require the opposing party to present evidence of chain of custody. If this occurs, you might have the opportunity to cross examine the laboratory technician, or others involved in the maintenance and storage of the evidence.

If the objection is denied, you will at least have an issue upon appeal. The alternative is to remain silent, allowing the evidenced to be entered into the case without a fight. The consequence of this is that you are now essentially stuck with the consequences.

There is a final form of objection you can expect to raise at a child support hearing. It is somewhat unique in that the objection is to the form of the question, instead of the nature of the evidence to be offered. This is the objection that the opposing party is asking a leading question.

This is the most common objection to be raised, as well as the most frequently successful. The reason has to do with the way in which child support hearings are usually conducted.

As we have discussed, these hearings occur in a hurried atmosphere. All of the parties involved are overburden, overextended, and usually underprepared as a result. The state attorney typically meets the custodial parent just moments before the hearing. The pre-trial conference is basically a hand shake. There is little or no attempt to prepare the non-custodial parent, or any other witness, to testify.

The result is that the testimony is not particularly smooth or polished. Just how bad things get depends mostly on the ability of the custodial parent to understand the questions and give the attorney what he or she wants. The situation is a little like someone trying to follow a strange dance partner.

It gets even worse when the custodial parent represents him or herself, of course. Either way, the trouble is that this improvisation often does not work. As a result, the attorney (or whoever is asking the questions), will often take a short cut. Frustrated by the inability of the witness to answer properly, he or she will begin to include the answer to the question in the question.

This is done by two methods, used either separately or together. The first is to simply include the needed information in the question, leaving the witness with nothing more to do than bob his or her head, or say yes. For example:

Q: So you want the defendant to pay one half of the medical bills of the child not covered by your health insurance policy?

A: Yes.

This is the "light" version of a leading question. The question would ideally be asked in a more open ended way. For example, it would be better to ask the mother "Are you asking for any relief as to medical bills not covered by insurance?

The Court would overrule your objection that the question is leading, although you would be technically correct. It would be considered a safe presumption that the witness actually wants this relief from the Court. As such, there is little point in requiring the attorney to repeat the question, with a slight alteration to the form.

As the testimony goes on, this becomes a more sticky issue. While the Court has a strong incentive to allow the litigants to "get

129

on with it," it should not allow anyone to essentially testify for the witness. When things begin to go badly, this can often happen. For example:

Q: Did the Defendant say that he was self employed, and always got paid in cash?

A: Yes.

If you are the Defendant, this is the point at which you get up and yell. As you can see, the question clearly suggests an answer. Worse, it suggests an answer that indicates you are underreporting income, and possibly involved in tax fraud. If you object to this question as leading, the testimony should be excluded.

Unfortunately, the damage might have already been done. Even if the Judge excludes the testimony, he or she has already heard it. There is no jury in a child support case, so the same individual who rules on the objection will decide the case. You have no choice but to trust that the Judge will honor his own instruction to disregard the statement.

The second method of "leading" a witness involves cues at the end of the question. Particularly when a witness panics and becomes unresponsive, the attorney will attempt to phrase the questions to lead him or her out of the woods.

Q: You saw the man pay him eight hundred dollars in cash, didn't you?

A: Yes.

Q: He put the cash in his wallet, didn't he?

A. Yes.

Again, you are standing up and objecting quickly. Again, the Court should properly exclude the testimony. Again, you have been damaged because the Judge has heard the damaging testimony. Worse, since you appear concerned about the issue, you run the risk of appearing guilty.

At this point, you consider additional options. Your problem is the fact that your objections follow the question and answer, or at

131

least the question. What you need is to short circuit the process by which this testimony is going forward.

The solution is to ask the Court to caution the attorney against any further leading of the witness. This should be done as soon as it becomes apparent that the lawyer intends to continue asking leading questions. As far as the question of timing is concerned, the sooner this request is made, the better.

With a little foresight, the problem can sometimes be completely avoided. For example, I once had several child support cases during a one month period. The same attorney represented each custodial parent. Before the first hearing, I heard a fellow lawyer refer to her as "the Queen of leading questions."

Since I knew what to expect, I was ready for the tactic. I objected to the first question of a leading nature, even though it only concerned the spelling of the child's middle name. I framed my argument to imply that I anticipated abuse of the tactic.

"Your honor, I am asking that the Court caution counsel about leading the witness. I believe there is a strong potential for abuse of this tactic due to the circumstances of this case."

The Judge agreed, and cautioned the attorney. I can speculate that he understood that this particularly lawyer abused this tactic. I was glad not to have to specify what "circumstances of the case" made me particularly concerned.

There is a good tactic. Few Judges will refuse to caution the parties about the use of leading questions. It has several positive effects. Obviously, it discourages the opposing party or attorney from using in the tactic.

Better yet, you put yourself in the same position as a smart coach who knows how to work a referee. By suggesting that abuse will occur, you create an inclination on behalf of the Judge to act upon it. If you've heard a football coach scream "They're holding," all afternoon, and finally get the call, you know what I mean.

If the tactic persists, it is possible to move for a mistrial. This is a motion ordinarily made in longer, more involved cases. However, there is no reason that the theory would not be applicable in a child support case.

Essentially, the argument is that the opposing party has effectively made a fair trial impossible. Usually, this is because the action has created inappropriate prejudice against a party. The prejudice is not based upon admissible evidence, and will have a serious effect on how a judge or jury decides the case.

For example, early in my career, I was hired by an attorney who had just completed a murder case. The defendant had an unfortunate nickname, "Mad Dog."

During the trial, the Judge apparently took a liking to it. He always used the nickname when he referred to the defendant in the case. As I recall, the Judge used the name "Mad Dog" fifty or sixty times total during the trial.

The jury no doubt assumed that the defendant had somehow earned the name. Since he was accused of murder, this did not help his chances of acquittal. "Mad Dog" was convicted of murder and sentenced to death.

The conviction was reversed on appeal. This was based upon a single factor. The appellate court concluded that the use of the nickname had prejudiced the jury, and deprived the defendant of a fair trial.

If your trial spirals out of control, it might be appropriate to request a mistrial. This is a remedy that is seldom requested, and even less often granted. Still, the fact remains that each case is unique. In the right circumstances, the remedy might be granted.

There is another major reason to raise a motion for a new trial, or indeed, any objections. It applies no matter how distracted or adversarial the Judge might be. It involves the context in which Judges work.

Presiding in Court, he or she might seem untouchable. From the beginning, the courtroom has been designed to convey this impression. Consider the bench, an elevated perch from which he or she is poised high above the litigants.

However, Judges are vulnerable in at least two respects. Firstly, their rulings can be reviewed, and corrected, through the process of appeal. Secondly, if mistakes are frequent and severe enough, they are subject to discipline or even removal.

In other words, no Judge likes to have his ruling challenged. The fact that you raise appropriate objections will result in better treatment, no matter what the circumstances.

However, objections must be considered carefully. They are to trials what spices are to cooking. By that I mean that there is a tendency to over use them, which can lead to bad results.

Take your cues from the Judge. If he or she appears to be presiding in a fair and unbiased manner, make your objections selectively if at all. Make objection only when the evidence offered is important to the case, even if the question or manner of proof is inappropriate.

The idea is to walk a fine line between alienating the Judge with unnecessary objections, and allowing inappropriate testimony or exhibits into evidence. The good news is that the typical child support hearing is relatively short, with limited testimony and few witnesses. This simplifies the decision making process.

The key is to carefully pick your spots. Most Judges expect litigants to be skeptical of the opposition, and anticipate a certain number of objects. However, each has a threshold point, at which he or she begins to lose patience with repeated objections.

Remember, the Judge has a certain degree of trust that the evidence presented before him or her in authentic. He or she is usually willing to allow you to dig a little deeper, and examine the source of information. However, the Court is always operating under severe time constraints, and impatient to move the case along.

Constantly objecting to testimony and evidence is a tactic which backfires on those who use it. This trap can be avoided if the litigant knows what issues are in dispute, and consequentially, what evidence is important.

In a paternity case, for example, the issue might be the reliability of medical evidence. However, if the question of paternity has been resolved, the only important evidence might relate to the income and expenses of the parties.

By objecting to evidence with selectivity and restraint, you command the respect of the court. This, in turn, should increase your chances for success.

CHAPTER SEVEN

Review and Modification Hearings

In certain circumstances, a child support case will be automatically reviewed after a period of time. This generally occurs when the custodial parent is receiving benefits from the state. The reviews usually occur about every three years.

The process usually involves an exchange of updated financial information. This is often done through an administrative process. The state will notify the parties of the review, and request certain information in writing. The parties are given a set amount of time to respond, after which the file is reviewed by a state employee.

Usually, the parties are informed of the result in writing. If both are in agreement with the result of the review, an order is prepared. It is customarily executed by a judicial officer, replacing the previous order.

It is important to carefully review any materials noticing you of a review. There is ordinarily a deadline to respond with financial information. In many states, the failure to do so has serious consequences.

A common sanction is a legal presumption adverse to the party who failed to respond. In other words, the administrative agency, and later the Judge, will accept whatever information is available as fact. Since this will have been provided by the custodial parent, the result may be an unjustified increase in the payment.

The process can be analogized to a tax audit. If you have ever been through this experience, you recall the endless succession of letters. The majority of them advised you of legal conclusions and findings, how to challenge them, and how long you had to do so

The administrative review of a child support case works the same way. Expect a written notice as to the result of the review. It will inevitably trigger a statutory deadline to take some responsive action.

The state law summaries included in the appendix to this book spell out these deadlines. However, it is important to note that child support law is an area of frequent change. The best approach is to

140

review any such letter carefully. It is essential to be absolutely clear about what has to be done and when.

The process of responding to the result of a review varies considerably from state to state. Often, the non-custodial parent is simply required to file a notice requesting a judicial hearing. He or she will the present the case before a judge.

Elsewhere, the process requires a written response, explaining why he or she disagrees with the results of the review. If this is the case, the written response will be crucial. After all, it will be provide the judge with his or her first impression of the case.

All states have "trigger criteria" for a change in the amount of the support obligation. There is considerable variance from state to state. However, a change is usually considered to be justified by a substantial change of circumstances, resulting in an increase or decrease of between ten and twenty five percent in the amount of the payment. The appendix likewise addresses this issue.

In some states, the mere passage of time is a "trigger criteria" for changing the support obligation. In general, if the order is in excess of three years old, there is a greater likelihood that it will be changed.

Each state has a list of factors which will be considered in the child support review process, usually in the statutory code. The law is relatively consistent from state to state as to this issue. However, what differences there are can be crucial.

All states recognize a change in income as a basis for a change in the support order. Whose income is at issue depends upon how the state calculates the child support obligation.

If the state uses the percentage of income model, the only issue is the income of the non-custodial parent. Since the income of the custodial parent was hot used in the initial calculation of support, it is irrelevant to the issue of change.

Of course, if the state uses an Income Shares or Melson formula to calculate support, the issue is more complicated. Since any upwards of downwards change in the income of the custodial parent is relevant, some homework might be necessary. This is particularly true if the figures provided are suspiciously low.

142

It is possible that other sources of income will be considered. Certain states will consider the income of a new husband or wife, particularly if the non-custodial parent is seeking a deviation from the child support guidelines based upon hardship.

There is also the possibility that the income of the child will be considered. The majority of states will not typically do so. However, only a small minority of states wil do so. Where applicable, such statutes contemplate full time or near full time employment of the sort that would indicate that a child is entirely or virtually emancipated.

CHAPTER EIGHT

The Federal Role in Child Support Enforcement

The individual states have the right and responsibility to prosecute child support cases. However, the federal government has taken an increasingly more prominent role in the process. This is not surprising, and can only be expected to continue.

The federal role crystallized in 1975, when the Child Support Enforcement Program was established under Title IV-D of the Social Security Act. Under the current system, each state runs its own individual child support program. The federal program assists the state agencies by providing four major services; locating non-custodial parents, establishing paternity, establishing child support obligations, and collecting child support for families.

The program has grown extensively since that time. In 1996, the United States Congress passed bipartisan welfare reform legislation. A major emphasis of the legislation was to improve state child support collection services.

`The new legislation created several new and important enforcement mechanisms. Among these are the national new hire

144

and wage reporting system, and the authorization of tough new penalties for nonpayment, including driver's license revocation. The program also vastly improved efficiency, and cooperation among states. For example, it implemented a system of computerized statewide collections, and also created a system of uniform interstate child support forms.

The effect has been dramatic. The United States Department of Health and Human Services website trumpets a sixty five percent increase in national child support collections in the year 2000, up to an all time high of 18 billion dollars.

To a large extent, this expansion of the federal role has had a positive effect. Regardless of personal opinion, there is little or no chance that the federal role in the process will diminish in the foreseeable future.

To a large extent, the Office of Child Support Enforcement can be seen as a specialized equivalent of the FBI. By providing an element of coordination to the efforts of the various state agencies, it has dramatically improved results. It is far more difficult to frustrate the collection process by simply crossing state lines, like John Dillinger or Bonnie and Clyde.

For several reasons, it is important to understand the nature and extent of the federal role. The Department of Health and Human Services provides the following services in support of State child support collection agencies.

National New Hire Reporting System: The welfare reform law of 1996 requires employers to report all new hires to state agencies. The data is transferred to a national directory, for the purpose of tracking delinquent parents across state lines. The location information is then forwarded to the state agencies so that child support can be established and enforced.

The Department of Health and Human Services indicates that over three million Parents have been located through this process. The states have become highly efficient in responding to this data. The new hire with a child support arrearage can expect to hear from the state agency within a matter of weeks.

Streamlined Paternity Establishment. The emphasis in this area has been towards making the process "quick and easy." This makes perfect sense, so long as the system is intended to operate as a collection agency.

The law requires each state to have an affidavit for voluntary paternity acknowledgement. The state is required to publicize the availability and encourage the use of voluntary paternity establishment processes. Further, the state agency is empowered to hold the mother's feet to the fire. Mothers who fail to cooperate with paternity establishment can be punished through a reduction in their state benefits.

CHAPTER NINE

Going on the Offense

Under certain circumstances, it is possible to turn the tables, and bring an action against the custodial parent. The opportunities to do so are limited, however. They occur only in circumstances of fraud or serious misrepresentation to the Court.

147

The basis for such actions is invariably false representations as to the issues of either paternity or income. A child support judgment is a potentially lucrative thing for the custodial parent. There is a strong incentive to pick and choose among potential defendants, pursuing the most desirable financial option.

Therefore, it is no surprise that custodial parents lie about major issues. This happens frequently, just as it does in every other kind of litigation. Unfortunately, the issue is usually ignored in the rush to cede the moral high ground to the mother. The fact is that misconduct occurs, remedies exist, and the Courts have an obligation to address the issue.

To some extent, this is a reasonable instinct to protect the caregiver. However, the reaction tends to lead the Courts to engage in destructive stereotyping. For example, Judges commonly conclude that a father seeking custody or joint custody is motivated primarily by a desire to reduce his child support obligation.

However, extreme misconduct by the custodial parent is actionable, in family court and elsewhere. It is possible to obtain significant financial relief, even years after the fact.

This chapter is not intended to address the issue of parental abuse or neglect. Under such circumstances, it would be imperative to file a petition for change of custody. If successful, this would, of course, end the child support obligation. However, that is a topic for another book.

The subject here is the possibility of obtaining a judgment against the custodial parent for monetary damages. This can occur when child support has been paid based upon an admission of paternity, in reliance upon the representations of the mother. To a lesser extent, it is also possible when the mother has made significant misrepresentations as to her expenses and income, in order to increase the amount of the child support payment.

The "perfect storm" scenario for bringing such an action is as follows. The mother, or a state agency, files an action seeking to a determine paternity and set child support. The putative "father" consents to the finding, waiving his right to paternity testing.

He does this based upon statements and representations of the mother. His motivation is to placate the mother, and avoid injury to his relationship with her. He might well be hopeful of resuscitating

149

their relationship, or at least of a positive relationship relative to the child.

Some time later, he becomes aware that he might not be the father. This revelation may come after months or years of support payments. He is most likely hurt and angered, and understandably wants to know the truth.

He will then discover that a conclusive paternity test is no longer his for the asking. While state law varies as to this issue, the family court judge generally has the right to refuse to order testing after a finding of paternity is in place. However, if the testimony shows that the "father" was coerced or pressured into admitted paternity, there is a reasonable chance he will be successful.

Once that hurdle is cleared, he faces further challenges once he discovers he is not the father. These are of a personal nature, as well as a legal nature. First of all, he has exceptionally difficult choices to make relative to the child.

I have seldom dealt with a father who was not emotionally torn under these circumstances. In most such cases, my client and the

150

child have been living a lie for many years. The "father" is forced to choose between attempting to maintain a semblance of the parental relationship, and severing all ties.

To their credit, most of my clients have taken the high road and worked to maintain their relationship with the child. Their emotional and financial investment in these children will be returned many times over.

However, the "father" still faces a legal battle which is more uphill than one would expect. While state law varies, the family court judge is not bound to vacate the paternity order and terminate the child support obligation. This is true regardless of any misconduct by the case worker, state attorney, or custodial parent.

Rather, the premise is that the decision is based upon the best interests of the child. Often, the Court concludes that the "best interests of the child" lies in preserving the status quo, and its financial benefits. There is extensive legal authority to support this position.

This, of course, completely ignores all considerations of fairness. We might just as well randomly assign each single, childless male an infant to support from birth. There is a complete lack of an obligation as the common thread between the two.

So, what can be done for the non-custodial parent who pays child support for months or years, based on a lie? The initial hope is that the Court will do the right thing, and terminate the child support order. Even if this occurs, thousands of dollars have been diverted from the income of the non-custodial parent to support the child. While more charitable words can be used, the term "theft" can fairly be applied to the situation.

While it seldom actually happens, there is nothing to prevent the non-custodial parent from filing a civil lawsuit under these circumstances. The potential best defendant is the state agency, which has the deep pockets necessary to compensate the loss.

Unfortunately, every state grants extensive immunity from civil suit to its state child support agency. There is little possibility of prevailing against the state agency, or the caseworker, except in the most outrageous circumstances. Even then, the best that could be

152

hoped for would be to extend liability to the individual employee, based upon the theory that his or her wrongful conduct was extreme enough to amount to a waiver of immunity. This is an extreme long shot.

The viable action is against the custodial parent herself, and is based upon the theory of fraud. There are good reasons to look seriously at this option.

Possibly the best is the fact that the case will not be heard in family court. It will be heard by a Judge who is not wedded to the state child support system, and therefore more likely to see the swindle behind the alleged good intentions.

The potential lawsuit should be carefully evaluated by the non-custodial parent and his attorney. The urge for revenge cannot be a factor in the decision. The point is to realistically evaluate the chances of recovery, to determine whether the lawsuit is worth the cost.

If you know the financial situation of the mother, you should be able to make an informed decision. As with any lawsuit, you are

153

looking for a defendant who has substantial disposable income, and significant property. Ownership of a home, a second automobile, or a business is a good sign. Alternately, if you know the mother to have trouble paying her bills, and substantial debts, you stand to waste money and time.

If the information you have is questionable or unreliable, there are a few easy ways to learn more. If you have recently been through a hearing against the mother, check her financial disclosures to the court.

People can and do make significant misrepresentations on these forms. However, you can safely assume that her financial situation is no worse than what you see on the form. You can also learn a great deal by checking for property tax records in the name of the mother. This will tell you the value of her home and vehicles, among other things. Such information can also be obtained through the internet, at a relatively cheap cost. The service can be found by searching the term "asset check."

If you go ahead with the action, it is important to understand the elements of fraud. The common law action of fraud is based on a

154

legal standard which is consistent in most jurisdictions. It is defined as follows:

> All multifarious means which human ingenuity can devise, and which are resorted to by one individual to get an advantage over another by false suggestions or suppression of the truth. It includes all surprises, tricks, cunning or dissembling, and any unfair way which another is cheated. *Source:* **Black's Law Dictionary**, 5th ed., by Henry Campbell Black West Publishing Company, St. Paul, Minnesota, 1979.

The term covers a wide range of dishonest and unethical behavior. However, for our purposes, it is more instructive to address the elements required to prove fraud in a court of law. While there is some difference in how the law is applied from state to state, they are thematically consistent, and three in number.

The first of these is a material false statement made with the intent to deceive. The term for this in the law is *scienter*. The second is a victim's reliance on the statement. The third element is damage to the victim, primarily caused by his or her reliance upon the statement.

The first element is clear enough. You would first look for a false statement made by the defendant. You would then examine the statement or statement to determine *materiality*. Generally speaking, a statement is material if prior knowledge would have been likely to change your decision as to admitting paternity and paying support.

You might note that this definition differs from the one presented in Chapter Six, when we discussed materiality in the context of evidence law. A stricter legal standard is being applied here, since in this case the issue is liability for damages, as opposed to just the admissibility of evidence.

The second element of proof is far more difficult. Fraud is, by definition, an intentional act. While it is true that the failure to do or say something can amount to fraud, it is also true that there is no such thing as accidental fraud. It must be proven that the defendant acted, or failed to act, with the calculated intention to harm the victim.

In our example, the mother who laughed at the party and said "he's a big sucker, that's not his kid," is arguably liable for fraud.

Why? Because her representation to the "father" (here the victim) was untrue. Her statement proves out that she knew it was untrue, and was aware that the victim had relied upon it.

By contrast, there are many situations in which an individual might have wrongfully paid child support, but not have a liability case against the mother for fraud. Liability would be questionable, for example, against a mother who was dating several men at the time of conception, and indicated only that she thought she had correctly identified the father.

In this case, the father would have to argue that mother knew he would have insisted on the paternity test, if he had known she was dating other men.

As in this example, intent is proven mainly by showing a *motive.* The best argument here would address the desirability of this victim as a father, as opposed to other candidates. It would be persuasive if he had a higher income or a relationship with the mother that she wished to maintain.

The final element is damages. The monetary loss to the victim in such a case is self evident. However, it is not the only element of damages to consider. A creative attorney could identify numerous other areas in which this victim has been damaged.

For example, the victim has arguably suffered damage through emotional distress. He has belatedly learned that his child is not, after all, his child. Assuming that any emotional connection exists between the two, both have been traumatized.

The majority of states recognize intentional infliction of emotional distress as an element of damages in a fraud case. In fact, most recognize this as an act which creates liability independent of the fraud action. This is potentially a substantial element of damages.

There are more remote, but still viable, elements to damages to examine. For example, the "father" might well have lost educational or career opportunities as a result of the situation. Lost in the stereotype of the "deadbeat dad", is the reality of the young father who drops out of school, or lingers in a dead end job, to provide stability for a child.

158

When these circumstances are raised as an element of damages, it is often argued that they are "speculative." We cannot, the argument goes, know if the father would have graduated, got the promotion, etc.

That argument can be successfully countered by proof of good performance. The honor student can probably show that he would have graduated. The worker with the excellent evaluations can demonstrate the likelihood of his promotion, etc.

The truth is that this is a particularly insidious kind of fraud. It not only cripples the victim economically, it causes him to make life changing and limiting decisions based upon lies. Practically unique among fraud victims, he can never be made whole.

Absent the fraud action, there are remedies available in family court. These are no where near as effective, but are generally less expensive to pursue. For that reason, they are the better alternative where the mother is of average financial means.

The first is alternative is to seek to have the mother held in contempt of court for perjury. The definition of perjury is, simply,

159

lying under oath. The proof of perjury requires certain, but not all, of the elements of fraud. There must be a false statement made knowingly, under oath.

The issue of damages is irrelevant. The point is not, at least primarily, to compensate the adverse party. Rather, the purpose is to punish a party who has attempted to perpetrate a fraud upon the court.

Recently, perjury prosecutions seem to be on the upswing. This can be shown by the numerous athletes who are facing criminal charges related to lies to federal investigators. These prominent prosecutions indicate a crackdown on individuals who make significant misrepresentations for the purpose of financial gain.

It should be noted that the sky is the limit here, as far as creating bad blood and hard feelings. Whether it is worth the trouble depends upon your long term goals. Essentially, the worse the relationship with the mother is, and the more you anticipate future litigation, the more likely you are to be able to live with the consequences of this kind of litigation.

Obviously, you stand to lose whatever goodwill exists with the mother, once you file this petition. After all, you are calling her a liar, and pursuing a course of action that could result in her imprisonment.

What is the upside? First of all, you stand to be reimbursed for attorney's fees, expenses, and costs of the action if you are successful. In most states, this would include all attorney's fees, expenses, and costs throughout the history of the litigation, up to and including the action seeking to hold the mother in contempt. Depending upon the circumstances, this could amount to thousands of dollars.

Additionally, if you prove that the mother has lied under oath, her credibility in any future litigation is lost. I have seen the change in attitude by family court judges after a litigant is convicted of perjury. In effect, the tables are turned. It will take tremendous effort on her part, and a great deal of time, to repair the damage done.

These options are still available when the misrepresentation relates to something other than custody. There is no reason that a fraud case, or a contempt action, would not be viable in other

161

circumstances. A misrepresentation as to the income or expenses of the mother, for example, is still a factual assertion made under oath. If it results in significant financial damage, it might be worthwhile to pursue compensation.

This approach can be your remedy for a family court judge who insists on preserving the status quo, in spite of considerations of fairness. For example, where a mother continues to receive child support in spite of the fact that the payee is not the father of the child, a fraud action is highly appropriate.

The intention would be to obtain a judgment which would offset the child support obligation. The lawsuit would be heard by a new judge in a new forum, outside of the child support system. Still better, the emphasis would be on the bad acts and misrepresentations of the mother, a circumstance which might turn the conventional set of assumptions in such a case on its head.

When the misrepresentation relates to income or expenses, the potential return of such a lawsuit will usually not justify the expense. Of course, the higher the amount of the payment, and the longer it is paid, the better the return.

162

There is also the possibility of filing such a case in a small claims court. These are courts of limited jurisdiction, which handle cases up to specific monetary value. While the potential recovery is limited, the advantages are numerous. The cases tend to be resolved in a much shorter time, and with less expense. Furthermore, the system is typically user friendly, so that a non-lawyer can function with some comfort.

Since few jurisdictions have ruled upon the issue, anticipate a potential motion to dismiss any such case. This would be based upon a state statute, which invariably vests exclusive jurisdiction of child support issues with the family court.

The argument is that this broad grant of authority would preempt any civil action arising out of a child support case. However, absent a statute which specifically addresses the issue, the argument appears specious.

Any state legislature inclined to grant immunity from liability for fraud to a category of litigants would be taking a virtually unprecedented action. It would be reasonable to conclude that it would do so clearly and unambiguously, by specific statutory language.

CHAPTER TEN

Choosing a Lawyer

Much of this book is intended for the individual who plans to represent himself. However, there are many good reasons to go ahead and obtain the services of an attorney. The better you handle the process, the more likely you are to obtain a good return on your investment in his or her services.

The first consideration is how and where to find a local lawyer competent to handle your case. I generally recommend that a client seeking representation meet with at least three attorneys before making his or her choice.

This is because of the nature of the attorney-client relationship. Unlike certain other professionals, the success or failure of a lawyer is irrevocably linked to the performance of his client. A surgeon, for example, needs nothing from his patient exception physical presence and good insurance. The best attorney, on the other hand, will be completely hamstrung by the wrong client.

164

By "wrong client", I do not necessarily mean that the individual is a lacking in character, intelligence, or some other quality. This can simply be the fact that the lawyer and client are incompatible in some important way. A client who wants a great deal of involvement in his own case, for example; will not be happy with an extremely busy attorney who demands control.

Therefore, before making the first appointment, it is important for the client to consider his or her own expectations, and to what extent they are reasonable. No less an icon than Abraham Lincoln said that "A Lawyer's only stock in trade is his time." For the attorney-client relationship to succeed, the client must keep in mind that this time is being purchased.

In other words, understand that a law practice is subject to the same constraints of supply and demand as any other business. Once this is clear, it is relatively easy to deduce a reasonable set of expectations. Thus, if the office has plush carpeting to your ankles, the receptionist brings you coffee in a crystal cup, and the waiting room smells of old leather, anticipate high maintenance with high costs.

165

On the other hand, if the office appears busy and cluttered, the receptionist points you to a seat while talking on the phone, and the waiting room is full, you are dealing with a volume business. Expect a better price, but lower maintenance.

As with any other product, the idea is to purchase the services you actually need, at a price you can afford. Fortunately, the typical child support case results in relatively moderate attorney's fees, due to the brief nature of most hearings.

So what are the best sources to find potential attorneys? The best source, without a doubt, is word of mouth. Unless you have sufficient time to hang around the courthouse, observe the hearings, and operate as your own "talent scout", this is your best source of knowledge about how a lawyer functions when the bullets start to fly.

However, it is also important to remember that this information is only as good as the source. Often, the bitter client who blames his attorney for all of his problems is simply looking for a scapegoat. The ideal source for this information is other attorneys, or individuals who work in the court system. Alternately, question people you know well, and take all information with a grain of salt.

If this sort of information if unavailable, there are other sources. The best option can be a lawyer referral agency operated by the state bar. These agencies maintain lists of attorneys practicing in various area of litigation, and refer clients to them. The attorneys are generally required to maintain malpractice insurance, and to have practiced in the field for a certain number of years.

While the result is something of a pot-luck approach, the potential client is at least certain that the attorney is of good standing with the bar, and insured. It is possible to do much worse.

The final alternative is to find a lawyer through advertising. This would include telephone directory advertising, television advertisement, or increasingly, web-sites. In the past few years, the negative stigma associated with lawyer advertisement has abated considerably. In fact, you now see older, established firms of the type who would never have considered this approach engaging in direct marketing.

If this is your information source, consider the content of the ad. In general, information based ads that steer clear of the ambulance and dented fender stereotype are an indicia of quality and stability. As to the yellow pages, keep in mind that the size of an ad is only an indication of the size of the marketing budget, and has little to do with the quality of the product.

For our purposes, a particular type of attorney is needed. As you will notice, most of the major marketing dollars are spent to attract clients with personal injury claims. These firms might be willing to take your case, but understand that you case is not what they are ideally looking for. You can safely assume that their priorities, to some extent, will lie elsewhere.

What you actually need is an attorney who emphasizes family law. Generally, if they advertise all, these attorneys will have less conspicuous ads that provide basic information and identify their area of practice. Even then, the ad is highly unlikely to make any mention of child support defense. Instead, the indicated areas of practice will be divorce, child custody, adoption, and equitable division of property.

There is actually some reluctance on the part of attorneys to take on a child support defense case. There are understandable reasons for this. Like anyone else in a business or trade, the attorney is typically careful with his reputation. The problem with a child support case is that, even when the attorney does an excellent job, the client will almost inevitably end up paying some amount of support. To many people, this translates as "losing."

In these cases, victory can be a reduction in the amount of the child support payment, or simply keeping the client out of jail. It is very hard to get favorable word of mouth in such circumstances.

As such, it is best to ask up front whether the attorney is willing to accept a child support defense case. By doing so, you exclude the possibility of wasting his or her time, as well as yours. If the answer is a less than enthusiastic yes, you should still strongly consider whether your time is better spent elsewhere.

When you appear for the consultation, be prepared to help the attorney help you. This means that you should bring a complete copy of your file with you. If this is impossible, at least bring a copy of any court order currently in effect. Without these, the attorney is left to guess at your true condition, like a doctor without X-Rays.

There are differing opinions as to how to approach an initial consultation with an attorney. The principle school of thought, at least among those who write about the subject, appears to be that this should be treated something like a job interview. You should expect the attorney to persuade you that he or she should be allowed to represent you.

Having spent several years on the other side of the desk, I can tell you the problems with this mindset. Admittedly, law schools have produced an over abundant crop of graduates in recent yeas, which leads to a presumption that attorneys are desperate for business.

However, in the case of a successfully attorney, this is no more true than the commercials that claim "bankers are competing for your business." In all probably, the attorney before you has a more than abundant caseload. He or she is willing to take on your child support case, at the right price and under the right circumstances.

However, he or she also knows that this case offers a limited financial return, and is a potential major headache.

Therefore, the worst thing you can do is to begin the process by alienating him or her. In my own experience, a potential client who begins the interview by asking about my years in practice, prior experience in the area, or for personal references is someone I probably want to avoid. This is especially true when the opportunity exists to make better money representing somebody else.

This is not to say that you should not check an attorney out, merely that the process should be approached in a certain way. For example, every state bar, without exception, will provide disciplinary information on an attorney upon request. This is usually available on the state bar web site. It would be irresponsible not to take advantage of this information before signing a contract or spending money.

You can also get plenty of information from the lawyer, without seeming difficult or adversarial. For example, you might want to ask him about his experiences with the trial judge, or the state child

171

collection agency. The detail and nature of his answers will tell you a great deal.

For the same reason, it is important to consider the quality of communication between you and the attorney. After all, the eventual success or failure of the case might well depend on how well you function as a team. If he or she appears to understand your needs and expectations, you are off to a good start.

There are a few specific questions that should always be asked. To my mind, most of these would be directed towards how the case would be handled. It is important to know how much trial preparation to expect, and how much of this will be done by the attorney him or herself, as opposed to an assistant.

Likewise, if the attorney happens to have one or more associates, it is worth asking whether there is any guarantee that the person you hire will actually try the case. There is nothing that shatters the confidence of a client more on the date of trial than to see, instead of the veteran bulldog he hired, a young associate fresh out of law school at his side. Granted that the younger lawyer might be a pleasant surprise, the "bait and switch" nature of the transaction is unsettling.

There should also be a frank discussion of his or her expectations as to result. Usually, an experienced attorney will insist on covering this ground, for the sake of his or her good name. It is highly difficult for persons who are not experienced with the legal system to have reasonable expectations as to the outcome of a case. This is particularly true where their financial well being, and often emotions, are at stake.

If the attorney presents a more pessimistic picture than you might expect, ask him or her to explain their reasoning. There are two possibilities here; from which you need to distinguish. The first is that he or she is providing a more experienced, emotionally detached, and reliable interpretation of the facts. If this is the case, the attorney is being honest with you at the expense of a potential fee. Consider this as a substantial factor in favor of hiring him or her.

The second possibility is that he or she has a negative feeling about you or some circumstance of the case. If there appears to be no strong legal basis, you need to continue in your search.

173

Remember, for almost every legal situation, there are multiple, perfectly valid interpretations. None of them are wrong or right, until a Judge with jurisdiction over the case makes a ruling.

Once you have decided upon an attorney, there is the truly complicated issue of fee negotiation. While this is not always the case, approach the issue with the mindset that everything is negotiable. Unless you are facing an immediate hearing, there is always the alternative of hiring a competitor.

In the best of circumstances, you would negotiate a flat rate fee for services. There are many firms which have traditionally refused to undertake representation under these terms, However, if trial and preparation time are limited, and the up front fee is substantial enough, most will consider this.

This is not an option that the attorney is likely to suggest. Instead, you will be offered a contract for an hourly billing rate, usually with additional terms. If possible, attempt to sway the negotiation towards a flat rate. While this will require you to make payment for services up front, you thereby remove the incentive to

174

bill for unnecessary services. The likelihood is that you will save money.

Often, the attorney will agree to this kind of arrangement, with certain added provisions to the contract. For example, he or she might require that the contract specify that the retainer is for appearance at a single hearing only, or specify that he or she retains the right to be relieved as counsel following the hearing.

These provisions should be carefully considered. There are many types of child support actions in which a "one and done" contract for representation can cause real problems for the client. The obvious examples would be cases in which the client is facing the possibility of imprisonment for failure to pay support, or is seeking modification of an order due to change of circumstance.

It might be possible to negotiate a "ceiling" to the billable cost of the case; in other words, a total amount of expenses and costs which the total bill will not exceed. This makes good sense, provided that you are comfortable paying the maximum billable amount. Your bill will almost inevitably reach this ceiling price.

Lastly, you might be able to simply negotiate a price deduction in the hourly billing rate. The important thing is to do your homework before attempting to negotiate.

For example, I have seen countless contracts with Pre-Paid Legal Services Companies, which claim to offer a substantial discount. Generally, the billable rate offered to the "service" is one which the attorney would readily offer a client off the street. You must know the local going rate for services in order to successfully negotiate.

There should always be a written retainer contract. You should be presented with a copy of it on the day you hire the attorney. It should set out the following things with specificity:

A. Name of the attorney, or attorneys, retained.

B. Identify of the legal matter in question (This would include the docket number if case is pending, and names of litigants.)

C. Amount of retainer paid

D. Billable hourly rate, if any

176

E. Flat rate fee, if applicable.

F. Identify any and all expenses which are billable to client

G. Terms under which associate or additional counsel can be employed

H. Date of execution of the contract.

A frequent problem for lawyers is the situation in which a potential client appears for an initial consultation, but pays no retainer and signs no contract. Surprisingly often, such an individual assumes that he or she is represented. This is particularly dangerous when the misunderstanding continues until a court date.

While most firms will send a form letter known as a "non-retention letter", there is no guarantee that the letter will arrive before the court date. Unless you have written confirmation from the attorney or through the court, it is highly unlikely that you are represented. If there is any doubt, resolve the issue immediately.

Further, if you leave an appointment intending to retain the attorney, discuss a timetable for doing so. A lawyer is subject to a

177

rapidly changing court schedule, and almost certainly cannot guarantee his or her future availability for your hearing.

I have often had a potential client disappear for several weeks following an initial consultation, only to reappear, check in hand, the day before a hearing. .Usually by that time, I am unavailable. Even when that is not the case, I am hesitant to take on a situation on insufficient notice and "wing it." If I agree to do so, I am offering the client the right to purchase less than my best effort.

The subject of changing lawyers is worth discussing, because of the serious risks involved. There is an important distinction that most non-attorneys are unaware of. This is the difference between an attorney who represents you in a filing and pending lawsuit, and one who has been retained, but there is court appearance is required nor action pending.

The distinction here is in the amount of difficulty involved in getting out of the case. If there is a pending lawsuit, and the attorney has made an appearance, the process is by necessity more complicated.

178

This is primarily for the protection of the client. Because of the on-going litigation, the client is likely to need immediate legal assistance. There is the risk that a significant event in the trial process or the trial itself, might occur before a new lawyer is hired. The more complicated the case, the more likely that serious damage occurs to the client's case during the transition.

For this reason, it is usually necessary for the withdrawing attorney to file a motion with the court. The motion is referred to as a "motion to be relieved as counsel." The motion will be served on the opposing party, as well as the client.

The motion will be argued before the trial judge. Depending upon the circumstances, the court might refuse to allow the attorney to withdraw from the case. However, the request is usually granted; particularly where the client agrees to it.

The Court will then consider the circumstances by which the attorney will be allowed to withdraw. The attorney is, of course, on his or her way out of the case. As such, he or she can no longer be entirely relied upon to protect the interest of the client.

Even if the attorney does not request this, the client should always ask for a period of forty five to ninety days to obtain other counsel. This should be done without exception since, even if the new lawyer is already retained, he or she will benefit from time to adequately investigate and prepare the case.

This request will usually be accommodated to some extent. However, trial judges, operate under considerable pressure to get cases off the docket. If the case has been pending for some time, expect the court to offer protection for a shorter time period, if at all.

If the request is refused, proceed with caution. There is the strong probability that opposing counsel will seek to take advantage of the situation by scheduling the matter quickly for trial. This is particularly true if the case is being litigated by private attorneys.

Worse, the change in representation will often result in confusion as to where court documents, including hearing notices, are to be sent. There is a risk that your trial notice could be sent to your previous attorney, who will ideally forward the document to you with minimal delay.

To protect yourself, send a certified letter to the court clerk, and to opposing counsel, notifying them of where you can be contacted. It should provide the following information.

- Case name and docket number

- Name of opposing counsel

- Name of your previous counsel

- Date of order relieving your previous counsel as attorney

- Your full name as appears on docket

- Your current address

- Your current telephone number or numbers

- Your current e-mail address

It is no surprise that the use of e-mail in the court system has increased dramatically through the years. This is essentially inevitable due to the factors of convenience and cost.

Many jurisdictions have now begun to serve notice of hearing documents through e-mail. This is a risky proposition, as anyone with even a passing familiarity with the technology can tell you.

Unfortunately, there is nothing you can do to protect yourself from the possibility that a notice is sent to an incorrect e-mail address, except to make everyone involved aware of your **correct** e-mail address.

It goes without saying that you must be clear on what method or methods the court will use to provide you notice of a hearing. While your case is pending, you must check mail and e-mail on a daily basis. If you are temporarily unable to do so, make arrangements to have this done for you.

CHAPTER ELEVEN

Enforcement Hearings - Avoiding Contempt and Its Consequences

In life, most problems are manageable for a sustained period of time. It is only by neglect that they fester, becoming wildfires that consume all before them. Most child support situations are no different.

It is a real shame that most non-custodial parents take no action to protect them until they have a court date. At this point, the few options available are mostly dependent upon the ability to pay.

When I was starting out in the practice, I spent a lot of time talking to older lawyers. I befriended one in particular, who had made a fortunate working out of a small building he had constructed himself. He had never had an associate, and had gone long periods without even having a legal secretary. What he did have was a lot of insight into human nature.

He referred me my first child support defense case. The non-custodial parent was owed several thousand dollars in back support payments. He was facing a Rule to Show Cause hearing.

In my home state of South Carolina, these are considered civil matters. However, they can and often do result in the imprisonment of the defendant for extended periods of up to a year. There were serious potential consequences for my client and his new wife and child.

When we had lunch before the hearing, I thanked him for the referral. I was just starting out in the practice, and the fee was a big help that week. I asked him how he usually handled this kind of case.

"I don't," he said. .

"Why?" I asked.

"Because it's bad for your reputation. You always lose, and the guy tells everybody how his lawyer screwed up and he went to jail. You'll be referring them out too, once you have enough business."

After that, I at least understood my situation. Turns out that my client did, too. A few minutes before the hearing, he disappeared. That Christmas he sent me a postcard from Bermuda, thanking me for being there to take the heat, and inviting me to visit "anytime." As far as I know, he never retuned to the United States.

So, can an enforcement proceeding be successfully defended? The answer is yes, provided that the goals are realistic. It is necessary to understand what can and cannot be accomplished in a hearing of this nature.

First of all, this is not a good time to go on the offensive. There are many reasons for this. You are essentially being dragged to court, with countless other defendants, all with similar explanations and excuses. The Judge is unlikely to have any patience or time for a hard luck story about the greed of the custodial parent. Such an approach is almost certain to backfire.

Save the request for additional visitation for another day, when you have filed a petition for a hearing of your own. Likewise, do not make your request for a reduction in child support at this time. This is true even if you have a strong basis for the request. About the

185

best response I have seen was from a Judge who, in a mid-December Rule to Show Cause hearing, was asked by a father to grant Christmas visitation.

The Judge advised him that he would hear the matter. However, since he was raising an additional issue, all the other cases would be heard first. When he got back around to him six hours later, he had forgotten about the whole thing. Since it was nearly five o'clock, he stuck to the issues in the pleadings, held the man in contempt, and sent him to jail.

Instead, it is better to file any petition to modify the court order before the hearing, but schedule it to be heard after the hearing. This actually improves your credibility with the court.

When the Judge hears one of the typical explanations for failure to keep the payments current, he or she is robbed of the laziest rationale for dismissing it. This, of course, is to simply say "You should have a filed a petition with this court for reduction of the payment. I don't see where you've done that."

Often, I have seen a Judge continue a hearing, so that a petition for modification can be heard either beforehand or at least in tandem with the contempt hearing. When this occurs, the non-custodial parent has already won a victory. Instead of having a few minutes to argue his case before a harried judge, who is already in a steady rhythm of sending people to jail, he or she will have a proper day in court.

This is why, when it becomes clear that you will be unable to make your support payment, you must immediately file a petition to modify the court order. Even if you cannot afford an attorney, the advantages of just filing the petition are too substantial to forego.

It is also necessary to consider whether any obvious defense exits. There are few of them, and most are fairly obvious. If the child resided with you for a time, consider whether this is when the payments got behind. If so, you should argue this as a basis to reduce or eliminate the arrearage.

The same principle holds true for joint or shared custody situations. In the majority of states, proof of shared custody, or of at least exercising more visitation than is customary, is a basis for

187

reduction. This should be taken into account in the actual child support calculations. It cannot be, however, unless and until this change of circumstances has been presented to the court.

It is far more difficult, but not impossible, to obtain credit for benefits provided to the child above and beyond the court order. The practical reality is that most non-custodial parents provide at least some, and often substantial, benefits of this nature. Nevertheless, documented proof of paying for clothing, tuition, medical expenses, or other needs of the child might be credited towards an arrearage.

If this is an issue, it is essential to bring as much physical proof as possible. This is the time to dig through your records, and produce canceled checks, receipts, etc. If the argument is that such benefits were provided in lieu of the child support payment, time line will be essential. This is a further reason for documenting each purchase to the furthest extent possible.

Be aware that this is an argument that can backfire. The Court might be sympathetic if the funds went to pay the child's dental bills. However, this is far less likely if the money went to purchase a four

188

wheeler or a jet ski. Worse, to have even made such an argument calls into question your judgment as a parent, and discredits you with the court.

It is essential to at least examine the possibility of an error in the math. This is true even when the payments are made through the state. The computer programs used for this purpose are only as good as the data in them. Since the date is entered by lower level state employees of varying quality, reliability is questionable.

The same goes double when the payments are made directly to the custodial parent. The custodial parent is often a fairly reliable bookkeeper and record custodian. After all, he or she only has to maintain one file, and usually cares passionately about it. However, the custodial parent also has every reason to rationalize or misrepresent the circumstances to his or her benefit. This happens not only as to the issue of how many payments have been made, but more often as to timing of the receipt of payment.

If the support is being paid through the state agency, always get a printout of the payment records. This should be done well in

189

advance of any court date. Most agencies have a particular method for handling such requests, and often only do so on certain days

of the week. This is the same information that will be given to the Judge at the hearing. It is essential that you have a copy.

Before the hearing, cross reference your own records and proof of payment to the "official" one. Be sure to check for any sign of a modification of the child support order. This is especially important if you are aware that hearings have occurred which you were unable to attend, or if you have changed address during the period in question. Even if this is not the case, it is possible that the order has been modified without your knowledge.

The print out will provide a complete history of the case. It will provide not only a record of all payments, but also a timeline as to all actions taken by the court or child support enforcement agency. By cross referencing your own records to this, you can avoid any possibility of surprise at the hearing. If you are behind on your support payments, go ahead and do this before a hearing is scheduled. In most states, you will be provided relatively short notice of the court date.

The most common defense raised in these hearings is financial hardship. The more the source of the problem can be traced to factors beyond the control of the non-custodial parent, the better. If the non-custodial parent fell off a scaffold and missed several months of work, he can expect some sympathy. However, he this expectation is contingent on providing proof, such as his medical records.

He can also expect to be questioned about unemployment benefits, disability payments, and other alternate sources of revenue.

If the bad economic consequence can be linked to a choice by the non-custodial parent, the result will be different. This will not only be true where the decision is considered selfish or irresponsible, such as leaving the jurisdiction to avoid paying support. In my experience, it also occurs where the non-custodial parent takes a calculated but defensible risk, such as opening his own business.

In such a situation, the non-custodial parent can be expected to defend his judgment in hindsight. He might be successful by showing that the decision was made partially due to the increasing

191

economic or emotional needs of the child. Since the court is charged with protecting the "best interests of the child", the argument should be framed in this fashion.

The Court will not care that you always hated being a surgeon, and wanted to paint landscapes. However, it might at least listen to the argument that you wanted to get out of the medical profession to free up time to spend with the child, or needed more money to pay his or her medical bills.

At an enforcement hearing, legal counsel is essential. The personal freedom of the non-custodial parent is at issue, at least for the short term. Also by extension, he or she is at risk as to job, reputation, and material possessions. Still worse, he or she can expect to be scheduled on a busy court day, with little time to plead his case. Absent counsel, he is at peril of losing before ever opening his mouth.

Fortunately, the United States Supreme Court has clearly stated that a right to counsel attaches in child support enforcement hearings, where the possibility of incarceration exists (See Lassiter v. Department of Social Services, 452 U.S. 18 (1981)).Almost

192

without exception, the states routinely appoint counsel for indigent defendants in child support cases.

This means that the non-custodial parent should be able to obtain counsel one way or the other. However, the Courts will not necessary act to appoint counsel without a request. It is the responsibility of the non-custodial parent to show indigence, and to request that he or she be provided with an attorney.

This should ordinarily be done at the earliest possible juncture, if for no other reason than to give the appointed attorney time to adequately prepare a defense. However, in light of the clear mandate by the Supreme Court, it is unlikely that the request would be refused. The probability is that a hearing would be rescheduled to accommodate the request.

Prior to the hearing, there is an opportunity to negotiate. The state is free to forgive some or all of the debt in the process. The procedure is known as an offer in compromise. The custodial parent also has the authority to forgive all of some of what is owed.

193

This presents an interesting dilemma. In many ways, the logical thing to do is to raise as much money as possible. That provides the non-custodial parent with the ability to pay a substantial portion of the debt. He or she can then use this leverage to negotiate a discount as to the principle, or more favorable payment terms. This negotiating tact is used successfully every day, in every kind of situation.

Unfortunately, in order to achieve this, it is necessary to show the ability to pay. The risk is that convincing the custodial parent or the state agency of a substantial ability to pay will backfire. In other words, instead of an offer in compromise, there will be a demand for payment in full. The showing of ability to pay can actually produce evidence that will be used against the non-custodial parent in court.

There are certain things the non-custodial parent can do to prevent this. First of all, it is preferable to contact the agency representative (lawyer or case worker) or the custodial parent well in advance of the hearing.

At that time, it is plausible for the non-custodial parent to ask about the possibility of a compromise settlement. Without

194

suggesting anything about income or assets, the non-custodial parent can then simply state that he "will see if he can raise this amount," and inquire about a deadline for such a settlement.

On the date of the hearing, this might be impossible. Still, there are certain things the non-custodial parent should or should not do. First of all, avoid bringing large amounts of cash, or other valuables, to the hearing. This would especially include jewelry. It will be noticed, and the estimated worth will be attributed to the estate of the non-custodial parent for purposes of determining ability to pay.

Worse, the item of property will likely be seized as an asset. I once witnessed a defendant in a child support enforcement case have his Rolex watch removed from his wrist in court.

Secondly, if negotiation results in a workable offer, it is best to pay the amount through bank draft or cashier's check. This is actually a convenience to the state agency and the custodial parent. However, it also offers an advantage to the non-custodial parent, in that it obscures the source of the funds. This allows for some ambiguity as to where the money actually came from.

195

I usually suggest that a third party deliver the funds. Since almost everybody has a cell phone these days, it is usually no trouble to have a reliable friend or relative assist you. Again, the idea is to at least allow for the assumption that friends or family are involved.

While it is possible that the state agency or the custodial parent already has possession of your bank records, it is as least as likely that they do not. If you do have substantial assets, it is in your best interest to give them as little incentive as possible to obtain them.

It is also a good idea to have the third party stick around for the hearing. If the case does not settle, and the worst happens, he or she might be your best chance to get out of jail quickly. This is particularly important if the case is heard on a Friday, something the non-custodial parent should do everything possible to avoid.

As with every negotiation, the key is to be a good poker player. What might seem utterly reasonable in court one day, might be wholly unacceptable the next. This is particular true due to the fact that case workers and attorneys vary considerably in the attitudes towards custodial parents. Some will negotiate independently, while

196

others will give the custodial parent an absolute veto. It is important to listen carefully early on, to gauge the attitude of the opposing party.

If possible, I suggest making an initial offer of twenty five to thirty percent of the entire arrearage, paid immediately. In return, ask for a twenty to thirty percent reduction in the amount of the arrearage, with the right to catch up the balance in small, additional payments.

This offer is in a range that provides a substantial, immediate benefit to the custodial parent. However, it does not suggest that the non-custodial parent was simply "holding out" and had the ability to pay all along. In return it seeks tangible benefits, an outright reduction in the arrearage, and the right to catch up the balance in small payments.

The odds of success in this sort of negotiation decrease as the amount of the arrearage increases, and with the every subsequent enforcement hearing. Once the non-custodial parent is perceived as acting in bad faith, negotiation will go out the window and the offer in compromise will be replaced by a "take it or leave it" ultimatum.

197

Again, like a good poker player, it is important that the non-custodial parent be aware of his "hand." In other words, remember that you have a strong incentive to settle. In a hearing, the worst that can happen to the state agency or the custodial parent is that the unpaid child support remains unpaid. The non-custodial parent, on the other hand, might go to jail. Any manageable settlement should be seriously considered, even if the result is less than ideal.

If the case actually goes to a hearing, much of the advice contained elsewhere in this book will apply. Avoid personal attacks on the custodial parent or the child, and complaints of ill treatment from anyone involved. Affirm your desire to help the child, and describe the actions you have taken to do so.

This is the time to bring out cash receipts, credit card records, or other documents evidencing incidents of support beyond the court order. This is also the time to present testimony of any extended visitation exercised with the minor child, during which time there would have been additional expense related to the child.

Following this, you would address any inconsistency in the official record presented to the court. This would most obviously

198

include failure to credit or document accurately as to the time and amount of support payments made. However, it would also include the following:

    a. Any informal negotiation between yourself and the custodial parent in which the custodial parent agreed to accept something else instead of the court ordered payment, (For example: The custodial parent might have agreed that, instead of the child support payment, the non-custodial parent would pay the home mortgage for a single month.)

    b. Any informal negotiation between yourself and the custodial payment which allowed for the delay in one or several payments, the reduction in amount of the periodic child support payment, or the elimination of all or a part of an arrearage.

The issues of health or financial hardship would be argued last. This would be done by first entering into evidence any documents which prove the following:

a. Illness resulting in absence from work;

b. Temporary or short term disability;

c. Permanent disability;

d. underemployment;

e. Loss of employment.

The term "underemployment" refers to a loss of work hours and wages due to downsizing or other circumstances. This can generally be proven by a comparison of check stubs or other documentation of income from before and after the change.

If the Court sees validity in the explanation offered by the non-custodial parent, it will question him or her further. In the case of illness or disability, the Court will inquire as to whether there has been an attempt to obtain compensation. The possibilities include a pending application for disability insurance, a civil suit seeking compensation for personal injury, a worker's compensation claim, or an application for social security.

The purpose of these questions is twofold. Firstly, the response might be an indication of how serious the non-custodial parent actually considers the situation.

Secondly, it might be possible for the court to apply a lien to the proceeds of any claim for compensation, to insure the eventual payment of the child support. It is possible for a Court to order that the proceeds of such a claim not be distributed without prior notice to the custodial parent or the state agency. This allows for a subsequent hearing at which the Court can divide the "pie" between the custodial and non-custodial parent.

If the problem is not related to a health issue, the Court will seek to apply pressure on the non-custodial parent. The purpose will be to force him or her to return to the work force quickly, or find a second job to compensate for his or her underemployment. In such cases, a ruling on the issue of contempt of court is often delayed. Instead, a subsequent hearing is scheduled, at which time the non-custodial parent will have either obtained employment, or will document his or her efforts to do so.

Likewise, it is common for the Court to order the non-custodial parent to advise the custodial parent or the state agency immediately upon finding a job. This safeguard is in addition to the federally mandated procedure, by which employers are required to report new hires to the government.

If all fails, the non-custodial parent will be held in contempt of court. Without exception, every state provides for the incarceration

201

of persons who willfully fail to pay child support. The severity of sentence varies, but is commonly in the range of six months to one year. The penalties can increase, however, for repeat offenders or where the amount of the child support arrearage is unusually high.

In some states, a Judge will include in his or her order an amount that the non-custodial parent can pay to "purge" him of contempt. In effect, the payment of this sum is the equivalent of posting bail. The amount of the payment is credited to the arrearage, and the non-custodial parent is released. However, he still owes the remainder of the unpaid child support obligation, and is subject to being held in contempt of court again should he fail to make the debt good.

For this reason, it is important that the non-custodial parent carefully review the court order from such a hearing. If it does not provide a workable structure for catching up the unpaid child support, he or she can expect to revisit this nightmare. The only way to resolve the issue is to file a petition with the court, seeking the right to pay the back child support in a manner comparable with his or her ability to pay.

There are numerous other remedies available to the state. Most of them are of an administrative nature, with little recourse for the non-custodial parent.

These include the following:

- Seizure of funds from individual or joint bank accounts
- Seizure of federal or state tax refunds
- Seizure of lottery winnings
- Seizure of real property
- Seizure of personal property
- Suspensions of driver's license
- Suspension of professional license

There is a common thread to all of these procedures. Usually, a written notice is provided to the non-custodial parent. It will advise of the action taken, and indicate a deadline to challenge the action.

Failure to challenge will make the action final. Often, this is the case even where the action affects a completely innocent party, such where there has been a mistake in the identity of the property owner. It is noteworthy that the holder of a joint bank account is generally subject to the same rules in challenging a seizure as the individual who actually owes the support.

Many states specify a "trigger" criterion, based upon either the amount of the arrearage or the extent of funds in a bank account, which will trigger seizure. This information is specified either through state statute or administrative ruling. The information is included in the appendix to this book.

Obviously, there is a serious risk for third parties. A non-custodial parent should avoid listing his name on a joint bank account, due to the risk of seizure. This is particularly true where there is a substantial child support arrearage.

In the most serious cases, it is ill advised to put any substantial sum in a bank account at all. Few states provided notice prior to seizing the funds. Consequentially, it is not possible to write checks from such an account without serious risk. Worse, only a handful of states will even allow the non custodial parent to argue his own financial hardship to nullify the seizure.

If you are subject to a seizure, review the notice carefully. It will indicate the basis by which you might be granted relief. It should also specify what you must do to challenge the action, and how long you have to act.

There are a few situations in which funds seized from a bank account might be returned. The most common involves a joint bank account, in which one or more parties are not involved in the child support dispute.

Several states impose a statutory ceiling on the percentage of funds from such an account which can be seized. Others grant all affected parties a right to request a hearing, at which evidence as to the source of the funds is admissible. Almost without exception, the third party has the same limited time to request a hearing. If he or she fails to do so, all rights are irrevocably lost.

The process as to all other seizures of property is essentially the same. It is typically administrative, and the effected party may contest the seizure under highly limited criteria. The most frequently successful grounds for challenge are ownership of the property by

205

an innocent party, or an error in calculation as to the amount of unpaid support.

Other than imprisonment, probably the most extreme enforcement remedy available to the state is license suspension. This can relate to an individual driver's license, or to various professional licenses.

This is something of a "nuclear" option, as to which state agencies tend to show some restraint. Certainly, by crippling the capacity of the wage earner, this tactic does injury to those it is intended to help.

Again, the opportunity to challenge is limited. Absent mistake, the action will be cured only by payment of all, or an agreed upon portion, of the debt.

206

CHAPTER TWELVE

How the Child Support Obligation Ends

To most people, this is presumed to be easy. The general impression, almost to the extent of urban myth, is that a child support obligation ends when the child turns eighteen.

Unfortunately, the reality is far less simple. The age at which the obligation ceases actually varies from state to state. Furthermore, in many states, it is possible to petition the court to continue the child support obligation through college. The same applies where the dependent child is mentally or physically disabled.

Likewise, there is the issue of back child support. When the obligation to support the child ends, this in no way affects the right of the custodial parent to pursue payment of any unpaid arrearage.

Finally, the act of concluding a child support obligation is not always simple. If the custodial parent cooperates, this can usually be done by execution and filing of appropriate paperwork. If not, the non-custodial parent is forced to file a petition to end his or her obligation to pay support.

Since there is such a wide range of approaches, it is necessary to provide a summary of the law for each state. This chart specifies the grounds by which the support obligation is terminated in each state, and indicates whether the state imposes a duty of support through college.

Alabama	Termination of support at 19, or when child graduates from high school	Court may require parents to provide post minority support for a child's college education.
Alaska	Termination of support at 18 or 19 if child enrolled in high school or equivalent and residing with custodial parent.	Courts may not require either parent to pay for post majority college support.
Arizona	Termination of support at 18 or until child graduates high school, but not past 19	No statute or case law holding parents to a duty to college support absent an agreement, but will enforce an agreement between parents.

Arkansas	Termination of support at 18 or when child graduates high school, whichever is later	No statute or case law holding parents to a duty to college support absent an agreement
California	Termination of support at 18, or if child is in high school, then until child graduates from high school or turns 19, whichever is first	No statute holding parents to a duty of college support absent an agreement
Colorado	Termination of support at 19 or judicial termination	The court can issue an order requiring that both parents provide for the educational expenses of the child, but cannot issue orders for both child support and postsecondary education support to be paid at the same time.
Connecticut	Termination of support at 18, or when child turns 23 if enrolled full time at post-secondary educational	The court may enter an educational support order, which may be entered into with respect to any child who has not attained twenty

	institution	three years of age, or not later than the academic year in which he or she attains the age of twenty three. The child must remain in academic good standing and make all public records documenting course of study available.
Delaware	Termination of child support at 18; if child still in high school, terminates at 19 or graduation, whichever comes first	No statute or case law holding parents to a duty to college support absent an agreement
D.C.	Termination at 21 or emancipation	Minor children are entitled to support. Age of majority is 21
Florida	Termination of support at 18, or at 19 if child will graduate from high school by that age	Courts will compel postsecondary educational support upon a finding of actual dependency, but attendance at college does not necessarily render a child dependant.

Georgia	Termination of support at 18, or to 20 if child still in secondary school	Courts will allow financial assistance to a child who is enrolled in college, (who is not emancipated or married) provided that it shall not be required after the child reaches the ago of 20.
Hawaii	Termination of support at 18, can be extended to 23 if child enrolled in an accredited higher education institution	Courts may order support of adult children through college
Idaho	Termination of support at 18, or to 19 by Court order if child enrolled in formal education	No statute or case law holding parents to a duty of college support
Illinois	Termination at 18, if child still in high school, terminates at 19 or graduation, whichever is first	Court may order support of adult children through college
Indiana	Termination of support at 21 or emancipation	Child support order may include sums for the child's education at

		institutions of higher learning
Iowa	Termination at 18 or if child is still in high school 19 or graduation, whichever is first	Child support order may include sums for child's education at institutions of higher learning
Kansas	Termination at 18, and automatically extended to end of school year in which child turns 18,	No duty to provide college support absent an agreement
Kentucky	Termination at 18, or 19 if child still attending high school	No duty to provide college support absent an agreement
Louisiana	Termination at 18 or emancipation, if child is still in high school, until 19 or graduation, whichever is first, or if child is developmentally disabled and fulltime in secondary school, until 22	No duty to provide college support absent an agreement
Maine	Termination at 18, if the child is still in high school, until 19	No duty to provide college support absent an

		agreement
Maryland	Termination at 19 if child is still high school, graduation or emancipation	No duty to provide college support absent an agreement
Massachusetts	Termination at 18, or to 21 if child is domiciled with parent, or age 23 if enrolled in an education program	Courts can grant order of support for a child between the ages of 18 and 21 who is domiciled in the home of a parent and principally dependent upon said parent for support
Michigan	Termination of support at 18, but may be ordered until 19 ½ for completion of high school	No duty to provide college support absent an agreement
Minnesota	Termination at 18 or 20 if still attending high school	No duty to provide college support absent an agreement
Mississippi	Termination at 21	Duty to age of 21
Missouri	Termination at 18, or upon graduation from high school, or age of	Courts can order support to continue until child completes

	21, whichever first. If child enrolled in vocational school or college, to 22	education, or reaches the age of 22, whichever first
Montana	Termination at 18, or emancipation, to 19 if enrolled in high school	No duty to provide college support absent an agreement
Nevada	Termination at 18 or 19 if still in high school	No duty to provide college support absent an agreement
New Hampshire	Termination at 18 or graduation from high school, whichever first	Courts can order support through college under appropriate circumstances
New Jersey	Termination at age of majority or as determined by court	Courts can order support through college even if child has reached age of majority
New Mexico	Termination of support at 18, to 19 if still in high school	No duty of support absent an agreement
New York	Termination at 21 or emancipation, whichever first	Court can order support. However, a parent may not be directed to pay child

214

		support and/or contribute towards college education expenses for a child past the age of 21 absent an agreement
North Carolina	Termination at 18, or through secondary school or age 29, whichever first	No duty to support absent agreement
North Dakota	Termination at 18, but if child is enrolled in high school, until 19 or graduation	Court may order one or both of parents to provide support for children for educational purposes
Ohio	Termination at 18 or graduation from high school, but not past 19	No duty to support absent agreement
Oklahoma	Termination at 18 or completion of high school	No duty to support absent agreement
Oregon	Termination at 18, or 21 if in school half time or more	Court may order child support for a child regularly attending post secondary education to the age

		of 21
Pennsylvania	Termination at 18 or completion of high school, whichever fist	No duty to support absent agreement
Rhode Island	Termination of support at 18, or until 90 days past high school graduation or 19, whichever sooner	No duty to support absent agreement
South Carolina	Termination at 18, or until graduation from high school	Court may order support through college
South Dakota	Termination at 18, or 19 if attending secondary school	No duty to support absent agreement
Tennessee	Termination of support at 18, unless child is in high school, in which case support ends at graduation	No duty to support absent agreement
Texas	Termination at 18 or graduation at high school, whichever first	Court may order support past the age of 18 child is enrolled in joint high school/junior college program

216

Utah	Termination at 18 or when child graduates from high school	Court may order support to the age of 21 in divorce actions
Vermont	Termination at 18 or graduation from secondary school	No duty to support absent agreement
Virginia	Termination of support at 18; unless child is in high school, in which case support terminates at 19 or graduation, whichever first	No duty to support absent agreement
Washington	Termination of support at 18 or to graduation before 19; court may order post secondary support	Court may order college support in its discretion, based upon enumerated factors
West Virginia	Termination of support at 18, or up to 20 if enrolled in post secondary school	Court has authority to award college support
Wisconsin	Termination of support at 18, or if still in school, at graduation from high school or age 19, whichever sooner	No duty to support absent agreement

Wyoming	Termination of support at 18 or up to 21 for secondary education	No duty to support absent agreement

These filings often become far more complicated than would be expected. The custodial parent is usually not pleased to lose the revenue source, and will fight to retain it. Furthermore, in some of the worst cases, the custodial parent sees this as the last skirmish in the divorce process. As such, he or she files a counterclaim including everything but the kitchen sink.

A hearing which should be a rubberstamp thereby often becomes an outright renewal of hostilities. The non-custodial parent must recognize this possibility, and prepare accordingly. This includes some obvious protective measures.

Before filing, the child support account should be completely current. If this is not possible, then regular payments should be made leading up to the hearing. The reason for this is twofold.

First of all, if the payments are behind, there is a strong probability that the custodial parent will file a counterclaim. Often, this will be a request to hold the non-custodial parent in contempt of court. There is, of course, the obvious problem that the non-custodial parent is now facing the possibility of going to jail. Worse still, the counterclaim will affect his credibility with the court, and complicate the process of proving his own petition.

If there is a state agency involved, the problem can be headed off at the pass. This can be done by negotiating a settlement as to the back child support before filing the petition to terminate the on-going support obligation. The non-custodial parent should always attempt to negotiate a reduction in the principle amount of the support by paying a lump sum towards the debt.

The same considerations apply to any other unfinished business between the non-custodial and custodial parents. For example, if there is a divorce decree which requires the non-custodial parent to transfer property or pay debts, anticipate that the filing of this petition might motivate the custodial parent to act on those rights. In general, the non-custodial parent must examine all

219

areas of potential trouble, and act affirmatively to protect him or herself.

Of course, the petition should be filed as soon as the non-custodial parent is aware of grounds to terminate the obligation. The support obligation does not end automatically because the child reaches eighteen, is emancipated, or for any other reason. Rather, it continues until such time as the court terminates the obligation. Delay in filing the papers is essentially throwing away money.

This is particularly true in that the courts do not award retroactive reimbursement of support which should not have been paid. This appears unfair, in that they commonly award retroactive payments to a custodial parent to cover the time between the filing of a request for support and the initial court hearing.

The process of preparing for the hearing is comparable to others described elsewhere in this book. To insure the best result, it is necessary to obtain physical proof of every important fact. Naturally, some things are easier to prove than others.

For example, the date of birth of the child is a central issue in most of these hearings. Ordinarily, this will be documented in the order by which child support was initially granted. However, there can still be problems.

In some states, these orders are often handwritten. There is no guarantee that the Judge who wrote the initial order, and can presumably read his own writing, will preside. Worse, I have been involved in hearings in which the original order was missing from the file, leaving the court with no option but to request copies from counsel.

To avoid the problem, the non-custodial parent should bring an official document, such as a birth certificate, showing the child's date of birth. This is a relatively easy problem to solve. While this does not become an issue frequently, I have seen hearings continued on this basis, resulting in weeks or months of delay. All the while, the child support meter continues running.

There can be similar confusion as to whether a child has graduated from a school. This is mostly true where the non-custodial parent is estranged from the custodial parent and child.

221

While academic records are confidential, a school has no basis to object to a simple response for the status of the student. A phone call should permit the non-custodial parent to determine if the child is actually attending the school

Alternately, a local newspaper will answer the question, or a search of the school web-site. These commonly publish lists of graduating students, and are readily available. Again, it is far better to plan ahead and appear in court with proof, than to simply trust that the custodial parent and child will tell the truth.

Proving that a child is emancipated from the custodial parent can be trickier. However, there are two things which are pretty much universally considered to show that the minor child has "left the nest." These are, of course, the fact that the child has moved out of the home, and that the child has obtained full time employment.

As to the issue of relocation, this might not be enough is the new address is a college dorm, or some other temporary residence adjacent to a school. This is particularly true in states in which the support obligation can continue through college, or past the age of eighteen.

Again, it is relatively simple to prove a change of address. The easiest place to look would be a telephone directory. A city or campus directory might corroborate testimony to this effect. These can usually be found in a county or school library. As a last resort, it is relatively inexpensive to obtain this information through a private detective, or an internet search engine.

As to the issue of employment, this, again, is usually only a problem where the non-custodial parent is estranged from the custodial parent and child. Where the non-custodial parent has absolutely no information about the child, amateur or professional detective work might be in order. If possible, the best approach is generally to simply call friends and relatives in the neighborhood and ask.

A final issue as to termination hearings is any alleged disability of a child. Again, if the non-custodial parent is in contact with the custodial parent and child, there is little possibility of surprise. However, where this is not the case, the issue comes up frequently. The fact that there are many children who are legitimately disabled should not obscure the fact that fraud occurs in this area.

The likelihood is that a totally disabled child will remain dependant upon his or her parents indefinitely. In such cases, the child support obligation may never end. Sadly, it is not terribly difficult for a custodial parent to find a doctor who will provide a helpful diagnosis prior to the hearing. That is, if he or she is persistent enough, and willing to pay the price.

My point is that the non-custodial parent should be skeptical of any such diagnosis which is too "conveniently timed." I am always wary of a short letter advising that the child is permanently disabled, from a doctor who has just examined the child for the first time. While there might be other explanations for the timing of the diagnosis, the circumstances raised questions.

Without evidence to the contrary, most judges will accept such evidence at face value. This is particularly problematic, in that usually the medical documentation is not provided to the non-custodial parent until shortly before or during the hearing.

There are ways to deal with this problem. The first is to object to the document on the grounds of chain of custody. As you will recall from the earlier chapter on evidence, this is an objection to the

224

authentication of the document. While medical records kept in the usual and ordinary course of business are generally admissible, a letter reciting a diagnosis does not fit the description.

Secondly, the non-custodial parent can raise an objection to any hearsay in the document. Since the doctor almost never appears in court, he is not available for cross examination. His opinion as to disability should be excluded as a result.

The evidence may be admitted in spite of these objections. If so, the non-custodial parent should request an independent medical examination. The federal rules of civil procedure and those of every state permit this when the physical or mental condition of a party is in question. This would require the child to submit to an examination by a doctor chosen by the non-custodial parent.

If this request is granted, the hearing will be continued out of necessity. The non-custodial parent should always request that he child support obligation be temporarily suspended pending the medical examination. It is a long shot that this request will be granted. However, if it is refused, the request should be followed up

ROBERT W. RUSHING JR.

by a request for reimbursement of any child support paid in the interim, along with the costs of the tests.

The matter of a request for support through college is still more problematic. This is true primarily because of the fact that the request is often made by the child him or herself, as opposed to the non-custodial parent. The fact that the inquiry is primarily focused on the fitness of the child only makes matters worse.

It is my belief that all parents should do everything possible to assist their children though college. Whether a parent has the capacity to do so is another question entirely. Likewise, there is a legitimate argument to the effect that it is never in the best interests of the non-custodial parent to submit to a court order, at any time.

These hearings can be heart wrenching, painful affairs. I have attended them with parents who cared deeply for the child, and wanted to help. They had no choice but to litigate as a defendant against their own child, for the sake of their own financial survival.

There is considerable difference in the manner in which states deal with this issue. Some, no doubt to avoid the problems

Copyright © 2010 Robert W. Rushing, Jr. All rights reserved.

described herein, simply include a cut off age for support in the state guidelines. The cut off age is often somewhere between nineteen and twenty one, to allow for support through college.

However, where the issue is determined at the discretion of the court, the abilities of the child are central to the issue of entitlement. Typically, there will be an examination of his or her grades and school records. The discussion will extend to evaluative testing such as the scholastic aptitude test and the like.

A further issue is the capacity of the minor child to obtain scholarships or other financial aid. It is easy to fairly easy to understand how the process can open up old wounds, and irreparably damage the relationship between the non-custodial parent and the child.

Of course, the ability of the non-custodial parent to pay is crucial. There is another unique aspect to this kind of support case. The custodial parent can be brought in as a party defendant, and frequently ordered to pay support as well. The dynamics and competing interests make for highly interesting hearings.

There is an additional argument I have seen used with some success in this kind of hearing. There is no case law to support it, but it is founded on a solid base of logic. The point relates to the amount of control presumably enjoyed by the custodial parent in the child's school choice.

Where the custodial parent makes more money, he or she will often tend to suggest one of the more expensive schools where there are less expensive alternatives. This, of course, increases the cost for both parents.

It can be successfully argued that the custodial parent, who made the choice, should pay more of the bill. In support of this, it can be helpful to present information as to the cost of alternative schools, and their relative quality.

These should be reasonable alternatives, in context of the abilities and ambitions of the child. The court will not and cannot impose an alternative choice upon the custodial parent and the child. However, it can use the cost of a feasible alternative in determining what might be a fair support obligation through college.

The non-custodial parent should keep in mind that the child, too, has an on-going obligation. The child is ordinarily required to attend school on a full time basis, and make adequate progress.

The non-custodial parent who does not enjoy regular communication with the child should monitor the situation. If fact, I have often suggested that the Court order require the child to provide reports cards and proof of attendance on a regular basis. This provision in an order can save the non-custodial parent a great deal of trouble later.

Once the support obligation has been terminated, the non-custodial parent should still take a few simple precautions. There is the possibility of a delay in preparation or filing of the order. This is particularly true if the order is to be drafted by an attorney who works for the state, or worse, the custodial parent.

As protection, the non-custodial parent should request that the Judge issue a bench order. This is done to provide written evidence of the Judge's ruling. If someone drags his or her feet as to preparation or filing of the order, there is a chance that the state will continue to expect payments. On at least a couple of occasions, I

229

have seen men carted off to jail, rightfully protesting that their support obligation was at an end.

For the same reason, it is important to keep the order in a permanent file. The non-custodial parent should also keep any records related to proof of payment. This might seem excessively cautious. However, on at least one occasion, I have received a call from a state employee, inquiring about a child support obligation my client had paid fifteen years ago.

Keep in mind that termination of the obligation to pay on-going support does not excuse the obligation to pay past due support. The hearing might be an excellent opportunity to address the issue of back support, but the order must address this issue specifically. Otherwise, the non-custodial parent will have to deal with this issue at a later date.

230

APPENDIX

Review of Applicable State Law

The information provided in this book is applicable in a broad range of situations. However, the area of child support continues to be one of the few areas of law primarily governed by the states. As such, *where* a child support case is heard can be the single most important factor in determining the result.

Therefore, it is essential to have at least some knowledge of applicable state law. The brief overviews provided here are intended to address the most frequently asked questions, and major distinctions, regarding state laws and regulations.

Of course, this information is only current to the date of publication of the book. The establishment of child support orders, and the enforcement of same, is a highly politicized area of the law.

For this reason, state laws are subject to abrupt, radical change. As such, this material should be seen primarily as an indication of what to expect. The non-custodial parent should always do some follow up, particularly as to crucial issues such as the state method of calculating child support.

The best method by which to do so is to check the state government web site. Almost without exception, each such site has an area which addresses the topic of child support. Unfortunately, the sites are exclusively created to assist those seeking to collect support. As such, their value is limited for the putative parent who disputes his obligation

to pay, or seeks to insure that he is treated fairly when the agency runs the numbers.

What follows is a frequently asked questions page which addresses relevant topics as to the law of each state. The intent is to allow the non-custodial parent to anticipate what to expect in a hearing, and to evaluate any conflict of laws issue.

This information is provided in the United States Health and Human Services website, appearing in the subsection for **The Office of Child Support Enforcement.** Again, it is worth noting that the site is intended to facilitate the collection of child support. It is

232

written primarily for state employees who work in the field. Consequentially, it provides much information that is of no use to the non-custodial parent, and omits much that is of use. However, the site is easy to find, and a convenient source for basic research.

ALABAMA

The Alabama state child support system is state administered and county operated. The state employs the Shared Income Model to calculate child support.

There is a twenty year statute of limitations for collection of past due support. This is calculated from the date that the support payment was due.

When the state issues an order of paternity, it does not address related issues of visitation and custody. There is a rebuttable presumption of paternity after an acknowledgement by the putative father. The fact of marriage to the mother also constitutes a rebuttable presumption of paternity.

When the custodial parent, non-custodial parent or other witnesses are not available in a paternity action, alternative methods of testimony may be acceptable. These would include affidavits, videotapes, or teleconferencing in the discretion of the court.

In setting support, the state considers the income of the custodial parent and the non-custodial parent. The state does permit

234

a petition for support when the only issue is retroactive child support.

The state employs an administrative procedure to attach tax refunds in certain circumstances. The trigger criterion for filing a lien is an arrearage of one thousand five hundred dollars ($1,500.00), where income withholding is not possible, or the non-custodial parent is likely to acquire property.

Other methods of enforcement of support include the contempt remedies available in family court. An additional remedy is passport denial.

Title IV-D cases are automatically reviewed for modification every three years. Other cases are reviewed at the request of the custodial parent or the non-custodial parent.

The basis for a change of circumstances which would justify a modification of the support order can be demonstrated in the following circumstances.

- The earnings of the obligee have increased or decreased.

235

- The earnings of the obligor have increased or decreased.

- The needs of a party or the child have changed.

- The children have extraordinary uninsured medical expenses

- Substantial change in child care costs.

ALASKA

The state child support program is state administered and county operated. There is no statute of limitations as to the collection of child support arrearages.

The state method for calculating a child support obligation is based upon percentage of income. When the state enters an order establishing paternity, the court will not address issues of custody or visitation. Marriage does constitute a rebuttable presumption of paternity. However, this can be rebutted by clear and convincing evidence of non-paternity. For example, the mother, the legal father, and the biological father may sign a three party affidavit which will be sufficient to rebut the presumption.

Alaska uses both an administrative and judicial process to establish child support obligations. The judicial process is seldom used by the state agency, but frequently used when a parent seeks a child support order without the assistance of the state agency. The state will allow a petition for support when the only issue is retroactive support.

The trigger criteria for filing an enforcement lien is a two thousand five hundred dollar arrearage, or for the non-custodial parent to be one year behind on payments.

The non-custodial parent has fifteen days to request an administrative review of a seizure of assets. The seizure can be reversed upon grounds of mistake of fact or joint account circumstances.

Support orders are reviewed every three years in TANF cases. In other cases, the party requesting review must provide evidence that the child support obligation would increase or decrease by at least fifteen percent (15%).

The criteria for demonstrating a change in circumstances which would justify modification of the child support decree include, but are not limited to, the following:

- Obligee's income has increased or decreased.
- Obligor's income has increased or decreased

ARIZONA

The state program child support program is state administered. Operation is by state, county, and private contractors. Effective September 21, 2006, the state statute of limitations for collection of child support was eliminated. In cases where the youngest child had emancipated and three years had passed prior to September 21, 2006: if a final judgment on arrears was not obtained; then the arrears cannot be collected. If a judgment was obtained for any time period within the duration oft the current child support and there is a balance still due, then those arrears can be collected.

The state employs the shared income method to calculate child support. When the state enters an order establishing paternity, the court will not address issues of custody and visitation. The state uses a judicial process to establish the support obligation.

The state will not permit a petition for support when the only issue is retroactive support.

The state lien enforcement program is administrative in nature. The non-custodial parent has fifteen days to challenge a freeze and seize action. A basis for the challenge would be that the non-custodial parent has not contributed to the account.

There is a review of any IV-D child support case every three years. The review of a private child support action is triggered by the request of the custodial or non-custodial parent. The criterion for modification is a fifteen percent (15%) difference, up or down.

A basis for modification can be shown by demonstrating any of the following circumstances:

- Increase or decrease in the income of the obligee
- Increase of decrease in the income of the obligor
- Increase or decrease in the need of a party or the child

ARKANSAS

The state child support system is state administered and operated. The state has no statute of limitations as to child support arrearages which have been reduced to a court judgment. However, arrears that are a judgment by operation of law are only collectible until the child turns twenty three.

The state uses the percentage of income model in calculating child support. The state does not customarily address issues of support or visitation when establishing paternity. However, the state courts will do so when properly presented by the custodial parent or the non-custodial parent.

Support establishment is done exclusively by a judicial process. In calculating the support obligation, only the income of the non-custodial parent is used. The state will not allow a petition for support when the only issue is retroactive support.

The trigger criterion for filing a lien is any arrearage balance by operation of law. The non-custodial parent has ten days to challenge a freeze and seize action as to any financial institution

241

lien. The deadline is fifteen days for any lien against insurance company assets.

As to every IV-D child support case, there is a review every three years. The process of review in private child support cases is triggered by the request of either the custodial or non-custodial parent.

There must be a change in the non-custodial parent's gross income in an amount equal to or more than twenty (20%), or more than one hundred dollars per month, to justify modification.

242

CALIFORNIA

The state child support program is state administered and county operated. There is no statute of limitations. A child support obligation is enforceable until paid in full.

The state uses a shared income model to calculate child support. When the state issues an order establishing paternity, it will not address issues of custody or visitation. Marriage to the mother does constitute a rebuttable presumption of paternity. However, the presumption only exists for up to two years from the date of birth of the child. After those two years, marriage constitutes a conclusive presumption of paternity. A husband may move for blood tests within two years of the child's birth.

The state uses a judicial process to establish the support obligation. California does not allow a petition for support when the only issue is retroactive support.

The state income tax procedure is administrative.

COLORADO

The state child support program is state administered, and county operated. There is no statute of limitations as to child support arrearages. However, there is a twenty year statute of limitations on enforcement of a judgment, which applies.

The state uses the shared income model to calculate child support. When the state issues an order establishing paternity, issues of child custody and visitation are not addressed. When the custodial parent, non-custodial parent, or any other witness is not able to appear in person for a paternity hearing, evidence can be offered by alternative means. Persons may testify or be deposed by telephone, audio visual means, or other electronic means.

The state has both an administrative and judicial process for establishing a support obligation. The administrative process is used under all be certain specified circumstances.

These include cases in which a Colorado order which establishes a monthly child support obligation exists, or an order exists in Colorado which could be modified to establish a monthly

244

support obligation. Also, where the County director or designate has made a finding of good cause exemption from referral to the Child Support Enforcement Unit. Likewise, where the case requires paternity establishment, and involves one or more alleged fathers. In addition, where the obligor is incarcerated for a future period of

one year or more, or one or both of the parents is under the age of eighteen. Finally, the judicial process might be used when the case is a responding interstate case.

The trigger criterion for filing a lien is any arrearage. The non-custodial parent has twenty days from the date of the lien to challenge a freeze and seize action. The action can be challenged for the following reasons:

- Terminal illness
- Commercial accounts
- Social security
- Joint accounts
- Mistaken identity
- Accounts used for child support funds only

The state reviews IV-D cases by the request of the custodial party, the non-custodial party, or the IV-D office. In all other cases, reviews are conducted at the request of either the custodial or non-custodial parent.

The criteria for modification of the support order include, but are not limited to, the following:

- Increase or decrease in the income of the obligor

- Increase or decrease in the income of the obligee

- Extraordinary uninsured medical expense

- Substantial change in child care expense

CONNECTICUT

The state child support program is state administered and state operated. There is no stature of limitations as to unpaid child support.

The state uses an income shares model to calculate child support. When entering an order establishing paternity, state courts will not entertain custody or visitation issues.

The state uses both a judicial and administrative procedure to establish a child support obligation. The administrative process is only used when the non-custodial parent agrees to the amount of support indicated by the child support guidelines.

The state process for instituting and enforcing liens is administrative. Any arrearage is sufficient to trigger a freeze and seize action.

In IV-D cases, reviews are conducted at the request of either parent, but no more frequently than every three years. However, the statute provides an n exception upon a showing of a substantial change of circumstances. In all other support cases, reviews occur at the request of either parent.

A support order can be modified due to any substantial change of circumstances as to either parent or the child. Such circumstances can also justify a substantial deviation from the child support guidelines. The statute notes that a fifteen percent (15%) deviation from the guidelines is presumed to be substantial.)

The following circumstances can be construed as a basis to modify a child support obligation:

- Increase or decrease in the income of the obligee
- Increase or decrease in the income of the obligor
- Substantial increase in the needs of a party or the child
- Extraordinary uninsured medical expenses related to child
- Changes in circumstance not sufficient for modification if contemplated in the original order. No modification for child care expense necessary, because child care is ordered as reimbursement of a percentage of whatever

248

expenses are incurred and paid. Other reasons for

modification are custody and payee changes.

DELAWARE

Delaware has a state administered and operated program. There is no statute of limitations on collection of past due child support.

The state guidelines are calculated by a method known as the Melson formula. The formula takes into account the incomes of the custodial and non-custodial parent.

When the state enters an order establishing paternity, issues of custody and visitation are not addressed.   In Delaware, marriage to the custodial parent creates a rebuttable presumption of paternity. When a witness is not available in a paternity proceeding, the court may accept testimony through a teleconference. The state also notarized signature written documentation.

The child support obligation is established through judicial process. The retroactive award of support prior to the date of filing is within the discretion of the judicial officer. In such cases, the Petitioner is responsible for providing adequate explanation of his or her reasons for failure to file for support.

The trigger criterion for the filing of a lien varies. A non-custodial parent must be delinquent for a period of sixty days prior to the state proceeding with a "freeze and seize." The non-custodial parent has twenty days to challenge a freeze and seize action. This can be done on grounds including incorrect identification, no child support payment being past due, an incorrect arrears amount, filing for bankruptcy, or the fact that the case is not an IV-D case.

In IV-D cases, reviews are conducted every two and one half years, or upon proof that a substantial change of circumstance has occurred. In other cases, review occurs upon the request of the custodial parent or the non-custodial parent.

The criteria for modification of the child support award include the following:

- Increase or decrease in the earnings of the obligor
- Increase or decrease in the earnings of the obligee
- Increase or decrease in the needs of a party or the child
- Extraordinary uninsured medical expenses of the child
- Substantial change in child care expenses

- Day care expenses, new biological children in home

DISTRICT OF COLUMBIA

The child support system is state administered and operated. There is a statute of limitations of twelve years as to the collection of past due support.

The district uses a shared income method to calculate child support, figured on gross income.

When the district issues an order establishing paternity, issues of custody and visitation are not addressed. Marriage to the custodial parent constitutes a rebuttable presumption of paternity. The presumption can be rebutted by genetic test results.

The district uses both administrative and judicial processes to establish a child support obligation. The administrative process is used when both parties can reach agreement, and must always be ratified by the court. In setting support under the guidelines, only the income of the non-custodial parent is considered.

However, there are criteria by which the court might deviate from the guidelines. These include exceptional needs of the child, or circumstances in which the non-custodial parent needs a period of

253

reduced payment to permit repayment of a financial debt or rearrangement of financial obligations.

The trigger criteria for filing a lien are any arrearage. There is no specific time limit as to how long a non-custodial parent has to challenge a freeze and seize action. There must be at least two hundred and fifty dollars ($250.00) in a bank account for it to be subject to a seizure.

The seizure can be challenged for several reasons. Among these is the fact that the arrears are inaccurate, the custodial parent has been paid directly, or a seizure has not been applied to the child support amount.

The state reviews IV-D cases every three years. Other child support cases are reviewed at the request of the parties, but automatically in TANF cases.

The following might constitute a change of circumstances which would permit a court to modify a child support obligation:

- Increase or decrease in the income of the obligor
- Increase or decrease in the income of the obligee

- Extraordinary uninsured medical expenses of child

- Substantial change in child care expenses

FLORIDA

The Florida child support system is state administered and operated. There is no statute of limitations as to the collection of past due child support. However, the courts have the discretion to dismiss such claims as stale, based upon the doctrine of latches.

The state uses the income shares model to calculate child support. When the state issues an order establishing paternity, it does address the issues of custody and visitation.

In Florida, marriage to the custodial parent does cause a rebuttable presumption of paternity. The putative parent has the burden of proof in seeking to rebut the presumption.

The state uses both an administrative and a judicial process to establish a support obligation. The judicial process is used in foster care cases, change of payee cases, Medicaid only cases where the custodial parent or caretaker relative does not want the Department of Revenue to address the child support issue, judicial referrals already in progress, and cases previously dismissed. The judicial process is also employed where the non-custodial parent makes a timely request for judicial determination of support.

The state will allow a petition for support when the only issue is retroactive support.

The trigger criterion for filing a lien is any arrearage as to real property, a six hundred dollar arrearage as to personal property.

There is a twenty one day time limit to challenge a seize and freeze action. The non-custodial parent may request a judicial or an administrative hearing, but not both. A non-debtor has the same appellate rights as the obligor.

The custodial and non-custodial parents are notified of their right to apply for a review every three years in Title IV-D cases. Non-public assistance cases are reviewed upon the request of either parent. Public assistance cases are reviewed every three years.

The following might constitute sufficient change of circumstances to allow a court to modify the child support obligation:

- Increase or decrease in the income of the obligor

- Increase or decrease in the income of the obligee

- Increase or decrease in the needs of a parent or child

- Extraordinary uninsured medical expenses of child

- Substantial change in child care expenses

- Any other substantial change in need or ability to pay

GEORGIA

The state child support system is state administered and state operated. However, some aspects are county operated. There is no statute of limitations for child support or spousal support for orders issued after July 1, 1997.

The state of Georgia uses a shared income model to calculate child support. When the state enters an order of paternity, it does not address issues of custody or visitation.

The state uses both an administrative and a judicial process to establish a child support obligation. In circuits where court time is limited, the administrative process is used. Each circuit determines whether to use the judicial or administrative process at its option. The administrative process is used for a wide range of purposes including paternity and support order establishment, and enforcement tools including income withholding, license suspension, and liens.

The state does not allow a petition for support where the only issue is retroactive support.

The state lien process is both administrative and judicial. A non-custodial parent has ten days to challenge a freeze and seize action, and must do so in writing. The states grounds for a successful challenge include mistake of identity or delinquent amount.

The state reviews IV-D cases every three years. Parents must show a substantial change of circumstances for more frequent reviews. Other cases are reviewed upon request of the parties.

The review process can be described as follows. Parties are provided notice of the review, and instructed to provide financial information. This information is applied to factors including the number of children for whom support is provided, and any special circumstances which would require a deviation from the guidelines. The result must amount to a fifteen to twenty five percent minimum requirement for an increase or decrease in order to justify modification. The agency recommendation is sent to the Office of State Administrative Hearings for administrative orders, or to the court for judicial review. Parties are notified and provided a right to contest.

A change of circumstance which is the basis for changing a child support order must be expected to last at least one year. The change must also be involuntarily. A disability must be medically verified.

HAWAII

The child support system is state administered and operated. There is an applicable statute of limitations for the collection of past due support. This is the thirty third birthday of the child, or ten years after the judgment was entered, whichever is later.

The state employs the Melson formula to calculate child support. When the state entered an order establishing paternity, issues of custody and visitation are also addressed. However, this is at the discretion of the court, and usually occurs where the issues are not contested.

Marriage to the custodial parent constitutes a rebuttable presumption of paternity. Also, if the child is born within three hundred days after the marriage is terminated, there is a rebuttable presumption of paternity. This also applies if the parties have married and the father has acknowledged paternity. If the father is named on the birth certificate with his consent, the presumption applies. Likewise, there is a rebuttable presumption of paternity where the child is a minor, the father receives him or her into his home, and openly holds himself out to be the natural father.

262

The state uses both an administrative and a judicial process to establish a support obligation. The state will allow a petition for support when the only issue is retroactive support.

The trigger criterion for filing of a lien is any arrearage. There are no penalties for incorrect seizures.

The state reviews IN-D cases upon receipt of a request. The review process can be described as follows. When a request is received with complete information, a notice of review is sent to both parties. After thirty days, a proposed administrative order is generated.

A resulting administrative order is served on both parties, who have thirty days to request a hearing. If no request is received, the order if filed with the court. If a hearing is requested, one is scheduled with the court. A ten percent change in the support amount is sufficient grounds for modification of the order.

Idaho

The Idaho child support system is state administered and operated. There is a statute of limitations which applies to child support enforcement actions. Any enforcement action must be commenced prior to the youngest child's twenty-third birthday.

The state uses the shared income model to calculate child support. When the state issues an order establishing paternity, it does not address issues of custody and visitation.

Marriage to the custodial parent does constitute a rebuttable presumption of paternity. This is rebuttable through genetic testing.

The state uses a judicial process to establish the support obligation. However, the parties are free to stipulate in order to save attorney's fees. The state will allow a petition for support when the only issue is retroactive support.

The trigger criteria for filing of a lien is a two thousand dollar arrearage or an obligation that is ninety days past due. The non-custodial parent has fourteen days to request an administrative hearing as to any seizure.

The seizure can be challenged upon grounds including the amount of arrears, the validity of the order, or the extent of the obligor's interest in the asset. Finally, the state homestead exemption can be raised as a defense.

ILLINOIS

The child support system is state administered and operated. There is currently no statute of limitations as to the enforcement of past due child support. However, any child support judgment that expired prior to July 1, 1997 may not be enforced.

The state uses the percentage income model to calculate child support. When the state issues an order establishing paternity, it does not address issues of custody and visitation.

Marriage to the custodial parent constitutes a rebuttable presumption of paternity. When the custodial or non-custodial parent, or another witness, is unavailable for a paternity hearing, evidence may be admitted in written or videotaped form. The court may also allow evidence through teleconferencing.

The state uses an administrative and a judicial process to establish a support obligation. The judicial process is used in all cases with unusual circumstances, and also in any case in which the circuit court has taken jurisdiction and the order has active terms.

The state will not allow a petition for support when the only issue is retroactive support.

The criterion for filing a lien is a one thousand dollar arrearage for personal property, or a ten thousand dollar arrearage for real property. The obligor has fifteen days to challenge a freeze and seize action.

The review of an IV-D case occurs every three years. In private support cases, review occurs at the request of either party. The criterion for modification is at least a twenty percent (20%) change in income, resulting in an adjustment of at least ten ($10.00) dollars per month.

The grounds for modification include the following:

- Increase or decrease in income of obligor or obligee
- Change in needs of a party or the child
- Change in child care expenses
- Medical insurance was not addressed
- Case previously selected for review but closed

INDIANA

The Indiana system is state administered and county operated. There is an applicable statute of limitations as to past due support, which is ten years after the age of eighteen or date of emancipation, whichever is earlier. The statute of limitations to enforce a child support judgment is twenty years.

The state uses the income shares model to calculate child support. When the state enters an order establishing paternity, issues of custody and visitation are also addressed.

Marriage to the custodial parent does constitute a rebuttable presumption of paternity. This presumption can be rebutted by genetic testing result.

It is possible to make arrangements to present the testimony of witnesses unavailable for trial at paternity hearings. There are no uniform procedures.

The state uses a judicial procedure to establish a support obligation. Indiana will establish support orders for prior periods.

The state administrative lien procedure is administrative and judicial. The non-custodial parent has a period of twenty days from the date of notice to appeal a seizure.

Basis for an appeal would include the fact that the funds in an account do not belong to the non-custodial parent, or that the non-custodial parent does not owe the arrearage.

Title IV-D cases are reviewed every three years, if requested. Other reviews are only performed upon request. The circumstances which would justify modification include increase or decrease in the income of either parent, extraordinary uninsured medical expense of the child, or substantial change in the needs of a parent or the child.

IOWA

The child support system is state administered and operated. There is no statute of limitations after July 1, 1997. Prior to July 1, 1997, the statute of limitations was twenty years from the date of each support installment.

The state uses the shared income model to calculate child support. When the state enters an order establishing paternity, it does not address issues of custody and visitation.

Most actions to establish child support are administrative. However, a judicial process is used when a non-custodial parent is a minor or imprisoned. The state will allow a petition for child support when the request is only retroactive.

The trigger criterion for filing a lien is an automatic judgment in the County where the support order is final. The non-custodial parent has ten business days from the date of a freeze and seizes notice to contact the child support recovery unit and challenge the action.

The action can be challenged on the basis of mistaken fact, including but not limited to a mistake in identity of the obligor or a mistake in the amount of delinquent support due.

An IV-D case is reviewed every two years, upon request. Other cases are reviewed for modification upon the request of either parent, or a third party such as a caretaker.

A basis for modification can be shown by demonstrating an increase or decrease in the income of either parent, an increase or decrease in the needs of a parent or the child, extraordinary uninsured medical expenses of the child, or a substantial change in child care expenses.

The order may also be modified for other reasons. A child may be added to the order. Medical insurance provisions may be added. This can also occur due to cost of living increases where the parties have agree to cost of living alteration.

KANSAS

The state child support program is state administered and operated. There is a statute of limitations as to past due support. Generally, installments due after 7/01/81 are enforceable until two years after the child is emancipated. However, with appropriate actions, enforcement may be extended indefinitely. Installments due before7/01/81 may be enforceable, but require case by case determination. In a proceeding for arrearages, the statute of limitation under the laws of Kansas or of the state issuing the order, whichever is longer, applies.

Kansas uses the shared income method of calculating child support. The state addresses issues of child custody and visitation when it enters an order of paternity.

There is a rebuttable presumption of paternity based upon marriage. This is rebuttable through genetic testing.

The state uses a judicial process exclusively to establish a child support order. A petition for child support is allowed where the only issue is retroactive support.

The trigger criterion for filing a lien is any unpaid installment. The non-custodial parent has sixty days to challenge a freeze and seize action.

A successfully challenge can be based upon a mistake in identity, or the fact that the debts is satisfied.

A Title IV-D case is reviewed as required by federal regulations. Other hearings are upon request of the parties.

A modification of the child support order must be based upon a substantial change of circumstances. Guidelines are applied, and adjustments are made in the child's best interests. A Kansas support order is automatically reduced by the child's pro rata share when a child is emancipated, dies, is adopted, or goes to live permanently with the non-custodial parent.

The criteria for demonstrating a change in circumstance include an increase or decrease in the income of either parent, a change in the needs of either parent or child, extraordinary medical expenses not covered by insurance, or a substantial increase in child care expense.

KENTUCKY

The Kentucky support system is state administered and operated. There is a statute of limitations as to collection of past due support. The statute extends until fifteen years after the last child emancipates.

Kentucky uses the income shares method to calculate child support. When the state issues an order establishing paternity, it does not address issues of custody or visitation. Marriage constitutes a rebuttable presumption of paternity. The presumption is rebutted by completing a rescission of acknowledgment of paternity form within sixty days. Written telephone, audiovisual, or other electronic means can be employed to present testimony in an action to establish paternity. This occurs at the discretion of the court.

The state uses both an administrative and a judicial proceeding to establish paternity. The judicial process is used at the discretion of the local child support case worker.

The state will not allow a petition for support where the only issue is retroactive support.

The trigger criteria for filing a lien is an arrearage equal to one month, with support having been assigned to the state. The non-custodial parent has twenty working days to challenge the action, which can be done based upon any mistake in fact.

LOUISIANA

The child support system is state administered and operated. There is an applicable statute of limitations with regards to collection of past due support. The statute extends until ten years from that date at which the child reaches the age of majority.

Louisiana uses the income shares model to calculate child support. When the state issues an order establishing paternity, it does not address issues of custody or visitation.

Marriage constitutes a rebuttable presumption of paternity. This presumption can be rebutted by filing of a petition for disavowal.

At paternity hearings, the physical presence of the witness is not required. A party may testify by telephone, or other audiovisual means.

Support orders are established through a judicial process. The state will not allow a petition for support when the only issue is retroactive support.

Support enforcement is by administrative and judicial means. The non-custodial parent has thirty days to challenge a freeze and seize action.

The grounds for a challenge include mistaken identity, error in calculation of arrears, or that some or all of the money in the account belongs to a third party.

A Title IV-D case is reviewed for modification every three years. Other cases are reviewed at the request of the custodial parent, the non-custodial parent, or the state. Both parties are provided with a thirty day advance notice of the review and an additional thirty day notice after the review to challenge the action. If the review indicates a change in the amount of child support based upon the guidelines, the case is scheduled for court.

Application of the guidelines must result in at least a twenty five percent change before the matter is scheduled for court, except in a three year review.

The grounds for modification include increase or decrease in the income of either party, change in the needs of either parent or

277

child, extraordinary uninsured medical expense, substantial change in child care expenses, or extraordinary expenses such as special schooling needs.

MAINE

The state program is state administered and operated. There is no statute of limitations as to the collection of past due support. However, there is a presumption of payment after twenty years.

Maine uses the income shares model to calculate child support. When the state issues an order establishing paternity, it also addresses issues of custody and visitation.

The state uses an administrative and a judicial process to establish a support obligation. The judicial process can be used where the court has assumed jurisdiction over the persons and issues.

In calculating child support, the state considers the income of the custodial parent, as well as the available income and financial contributions of the domestic associate or current spouse of each party and a child's financial resources can be reasons to justify deviating from the support guidelines.

The criteria for filing a lien occur twenty one days after receipt of a notice of debt or thirty days after an IV-D agency's decision that requires a non-custodial parent to pay support. The non-custodial parent has thirty days to challenge a freeze and seize action.

The challenge must be based upon affirmative defenses.

In an IV-D case, notices are sent to parents every three years, informing them of the availability of the review process. Other reviews are at the request of a party.

In the process, income information is collected from the parties. If the new order would be fifteen percent (15%) higher then the present order, or there has been a significant change of circumstances, then the review proceeds. Court orders are reviewed in the same manner.

If the order is over three years old, the Court must review the order. If not, there must be a showing of a substantial change of circumstances.

The order can be modified based upon increase or decrease in the income of either parent, substantial change in needs, extraordinary uninsured medical expense, or a substantial increase in day care costs. Also, if a child receives dependent benefits as a

280

result of the disability of a parent, the court must give that parent

credit for the benefits paid to the child.

MARYLAND

The program is state administered and state operated. There is no statute of limitations as to unpaid child support.

Maryland uses the income shares model to calculate child support. When the state enters an adjudication of paternity, it will address issues of custody and visitation.

Marriage constitutes a rebuttable presumption of paternity, which may be rebutted by testimony of a person other than the mother or her husband.

The state uses a judicial process to establish a support orders. Only the parent's income is considered in the calculation. The state will not allow a petition for support where the only issue is retroactive support.

The lien process is administrative. The trigger criterion is a five hundred dollar minimum delinquency and no payment for more than sixty days for sole ownership accounts, use of the remedy by local agencies is discretionary. Accounts must have a minimum of two thousand five hundred dollars for a lien to attach to the asset.

The non-custodial parent may file a request for an investigation of the seizure for thirty days from the date of the notice.

An IV-D case may be requested for review every three years, or upon evidence of a substantial change of circumstances of more than six months duration. Other reviews are at the request of the custodial or non-custodial parent/.

Circumstances which may constitute a change of circumstances include increase or decrease in the income of a parent, change in the needs of a parent or child, extraordinary uninsured medical expense, change in child care costs, or the incarceration of a parent where this affects the ability to pay.

MASSACHUSETTS

The program is state administered and operated. There is no statute of limitations as to past due support.

Massachusetts uses the percentage of income model to calculate support. The state does not address issues of custody and visitation when establishing an order of paternity.

The support order is established through a judicial process. The state will not allow a petition for support where the only issue is retroactive support.

284

MICHIGAN

The program is state administered, but county operated. There is a statute of limitations as to past due child support. This extends until ten years after the date the last obligation is due. Affirmative defenses also apply in an action to collect past due child support.

Michigan uses a modified income shares method to calculate support. When the state issues an order of paternity, it will address related issues of custody and visitation. Marriage results in a presumption of paternity. This can be rebutted only in a court proceeding, and only if the putative father is available. Than and only then is the legal father excluded.

The support order is established through a judicial \process. The state does not allow a petition for support where the only issue is retroactive support.

Further, there are limits upon the collection of support for prior periods. In paternity cases, the order is retroactive only to the date that the complaint was filed unless the defendant was avoiding service of process, threatened or coerced the custodial parent

285

through domestic violence, or otherwise delayed the imposition of a support order.

The state enforcement process is administrative. Past due support in an amount which exceeds two times the monthly amount of periodic support payments payable under the support order will trigger the filing of a lien. The non-custodial parent has twenty one day from the date a lien is placed to challenge a freeze and seize action.

The challenge can be based upon a mistake in fact, a mistake of identity, or a disagreement as to the arrearage amount.

An IV-D order will be reviewed not less than once every thirty six months. Other reviews occur when a party requests a review in writing, or the state does so.

The criteria for modification include a "threshold for modification" of ten percent, or at least twenty five dollars per month, whichever is less. The basis can be an increase or decrease in the income of a parent, a change in the needs of a parent of child,

286

extraordinary uninsured medical expense, or a change in child care costs.

<u>MINNESOTA</u>

The Department of Human Services is the executive branch agency responsible for supervising Minnesota's child support system, which is administered by the county child support offices.

There is no statute of limitations of certain child support collection remedies including income withholding, state tax exemption, and credit bureau reporting. However, the ten year statute of limitations on judgments is applicable.

The state uses the income shares model to calculate child support. When the state enters an order establishing paternity, it will address issues of custody and visitation.

Marriage results in a rebuttable presumption of paternity. It is rebuttable by clear and convincing evidence, a court order establishing paternity of another or a recognition of parentage document signed by both natural parents. There are several other circumstances that result in a presumption of paternity. The first is any situation in which attempted to marry before the child is born. The second is where the

288

parties marry after the child is born, and the father admits paternity in writing, or is named on the birth certificate, and takes the child into his home and acknowledges him as his son. Also, the presumption exists where the child is born within two hundred and eighty days after the marriage is terminated.

In a paternity action, evidence by affidavit, deposition, videotape, or teleconferencing is admissible.

The state has an expedited process to establish, modify, and enforce support orders. When issues are outside of the scope of the process, such as custody, visitation, or contested parentage, the judicial process is used.

In calculating child support, the custodial parent's income is also considered. A new spouse or the child's income is not. A deduction is also allowed for spousal maintenance orders and child support orders for non-joint children that a party is obligated to pay.

The court may deviate from the guidelines if both the parties agree and it is approved by the court, provided that the deviation serves the best interests of the child.

The state enforcement remedies are both administrative and judicial. The non-custodial parent may claim exemption as to a lien within twenty days of receiving notice. This may result in an informal resolution regarding a mistake or exemption. The non-custodial parent may also request a hearing within thirty days of receiving notice. The non-custodial parent must set the hearing date with the administrative office, and serve the child support agency within two days of filing the motion.

Most Minnesota support orders are adjusted every two years. All parties have the right to request a review at any time. Participants are provided with reminder notices every thirty six months.

The support order may be modified for several reasons. This will occur when there is a twenty percent change in the income of the obligor; there is a change in the number of children supported by the decree; a parent or caregiver begins receiving public assistance; additional work or education related child care expenses; a substantial change related to health care coverage; the child becomes disabled; or both parents consent to a modification.

MISSISSIPPI

The program is state administered but county operated. There is a statute of limitations applicable to collection of past due support. The statute extends seven years past the age of majority of the child, which is twenty one years of age.

The state uses the percentage of gross income method to calculate support. When the state enters an order establishing paternity, it does not address the issues of custody and visitation. However, it is possible for the court to do so at its option.

Marriage does create a rebuttable presumption of paternity, which can be rebutted in chancery court. Paternity is sometimes adjudicated on evidence of blood tests alone in the absence of witnesses.

The process to establish a support obligation is judicial. The state will allow a petition for support where the only issue is retroactive support.

The state lien process is judicial. There must be a two hundred and fifty dollar minimum delinquency, for a time of over two months, for a property seizure to occur. IRA accounts are exempted.

The non-custodial parent has forty five days to appeal a freeze and seizers order.

A Title IV-D case is reviewed every three years. Other cases are reviewed upon request of either party. The request must be in writing.

The criterion for modification is a twenty five percent change in the ordered amount. The basis can be an increase or decrease in the income of either parent, a change in the needs of a parent or the child, or extraordinary uninsured medical expenses.

The state also recognizes a change of custody arrangements as a basis for modification.

MISSOURI

The program is operated by a combination of state and county agencies. There is a statute of limitations applicable to the collection of past due child support. The deadline is ten days from the last payment on record or other form of revival of the court order on record.

The state uses a shared income model to calculate child support. When the state issues an order establishing paternity, it will address issues of custody and visitation.

Marriage results in a presumption of paternity, rebuttable by clear and convincing evidence. There is also a presumption related to attempted marriage and legitimization.

The state uses both an administrative and a judicial process to establish a support obligation. A case is generally handled judicially if 1) it requires a UIFSA action 2) it involves a presumed vs. alleged situation which cannot be resolved through three party affidavit, 3) it involves a minor parent; 4) presumptive or legal parentage cannot be established administratively.

The state will not allow a petition for support when the only issue is retroactive support.

The state lien process is administrative. The trigger criterion for filing of a lien is a one thousand dollar arrearage for personal property. There is no specific trigger amount as to real property. An obligor must be delinquent sixty days before the state will proceed with a freeze and seize.

The non-custodial parent has a right to appeal the freeze and seize order for a period of sixty days from the date of the freeze. He or she is only entitled to a review of the arrearage amount. The non-custodial parent and any non-debtor have thirty days from the date of the notice to rebut the equal share presumption as to joint accounts.

An IV-D case is reviewed every three years, unless special circumstances apply. Other reviews are upon request. If a review is appropriate, financial information on both parties is obtained. The parties have the right to contest the motion to modify.

Modification is considered appropriate when the presumed child support amount differs by twenty percent or more. The grounds for modification include increase or decrease in the income of either parent,

<u>MONTANA</u>

The program is state administered and operated. There is a statute of limitations applicable to the collection of past due support. The limitation is ten years from the date payment is due for debt accrued prior to 10/1/93, ten years after termination of the obligation for payments due after that date.

Montana uses a modified Melson formula to calculate support. When the court enters an order establishing paternity, it does not address issues of custody or visitation.

Marriage results in a presumption of paternity. If a paternity presumption arising out of marriage is not rebutted during a dissolution action, it is not rebuttable. Prior to dissolution, the presumption may be rebutted by appropriate action.

There are other facts that create a rebuttable presumption. These include 1) alleged father and mother attempt to marry after the child's birth, and there is a support order against alleged father; 2) father receives child into his home and represents him to be his child, 3) alleged father registers with the putative father registry and mother does not deny that he is father.

The support order is established by an administrative process. Income of both parents is considered in calculating support. Income of a child or new spouse can be considered as to deviation from the guidelines.

The enforcement process is also administrative. The trigger criterion for filing of a lien is a delinquency greater than one hundred and fifty dollars, unenforceable by income withholding. The value of the property must exceed the value of any exemptions, and the amount of any superior liens.

The non-custodial parent has ten working days from receipt of notice to challenge a freeze and seize order. The challenge may involve whether the property in question is subject to an exemption, the validity of the judgment, and whether payments have been made since filing of the lien.

An IV-D case is reviewed every thirty six months, or when a significant change of circumstances occurs. Other cases are reviewed upon request.

The process is a multi staged administrative proceeding, with the possibility of a contested case hearing, and subsequent judicial review. To justify modification, the resulting increase or decrease must be in excess of twenty five dollars per month. The modified support order must require the non-custodial parent to obtain health insurance if available if not included in the previous order. The modified order must provide credit for social security benefits paid to the child as a result of the non-custodial parent's disability.

Other grounds for modification exist. These include 1) change in custody/extended visitation; 2) emancipation of a child, or death 3) child born to parents after entry of previous order; 4) non-custodial parent has become disabled or rehabilitated.

NEBRASKA

The program is administered and operated by the state and counties. There is no statue of limitations as to the collection of unpaid child support.

Nebraska uses a shared income model to calculate support. When the state enters an order establishing paternity, it will address issues of custody and visitation. This will occur if the parties are represented by their own counsel and wish to do so.

Marriage results in a presumption of paternity, rebuttable by court action.

The support order is established judicially. The child support guidelines are strictly applied, unless the court finds that one or both of the parties have produced sufficient evidence to show that the result will not be fair or equitable. The state will not allow a petition for support where the only issue is retroactive support.

The enforcement mechanism is administrative and judicial. The trigger criteria for filing a lien is a delinquency in the child support obligation.

299

An IV-D case I s reviewed upon request but no more often than every three years. Other reviews are by state agency request, or that of either the custodial or non-custodial parent,

A review of modification packet is sent to the requesting party. Once the information is received, a notice is sent to the non-requesting party, who has thirty days to respond. After thirty days, a review determination notice is sent to both parties, stating whether or not the case will be referred to the county attorney to file a petition for modification of support. This will occur where 1) there is a ten percent change, upwards or downwards; 2) health insurance is newly available; 3) failure to provide sufficient information by the non-custodial parent creates a rebuttable presumption.

Upon receipt of the notice, each party has thirty days to submit a written request for consideration to the court stating why he or she agrees or disagrees with the review determination. Once referred to the county attorney, the attorney decided whether or not to file in court.

NEVADA

The program is administered by a combination of state and county agencies. There is no statute of limitations if an order exists. Retroactive support may be requested back four years from the date of application for services.

The state uses a percentage of income model to calculate support. The court will not address issues of custody or visitation when it enters an order establishing paternity.

Marriage creates a presumption of legitimacy, rebuttable for six month after which it becomes conclusive.

There is also a presumption under certain other circumstances. These include 1) cohabiting six months prior to and through the period of conception; 2) attempted marriage; 3) alleged father receives the child in his home and hold him or her out to be his child. Written testimony, teleconferencing, and audio-visual means can be used to present testimony.

The support order is established by a quasi-judicial process. The state will not allow a petition for support where the only issue is retroactive support.

The trigger criteria for filing a lien is any child support arrearage. The non-custodial parent has twenty days to challenge a freeze and seize action. The seizure is triggered by a minimum delinquency of five thousand dollars, which is lowered to one thousand dollars in state support cases.

A title IV-D case is reviewed every three years. Other cases are reviewed upon written request of a party, or the state agency.

A case manager reviews the file, to determine whether the case meets change of circumstance criteria. This must occur within one hundred and eighty days of receipt of the request. The case manager must notify the parties of the proposed adjustment and their right to request a hearing to challenge the decision.

There are further criteria. The order 1) must be at least thirty six months old; 2) the modification must result in a fifteen percent increase or decrease, or a seventy five dollar increase or decrease; 3) or health insurance must be newly available.

If the request is based on change of circumstances, and the three year rule does not apply, there must be at least a twenty percent change in the gross monthly income of a person who is the subject of the order for support.

NEW HAMPSHIRE

The program is state administered and operated. There is a statute of limitations applicable to the collection of unpaid child support. Support payments become judgments when due, with a statute of limitations of twenty years.

New Hampshire uses an income shares formula to calculate support. The state does not address issues of custody or visitation when entering an adjudication of paternity. Marriage constitutes a rebuttable presumption of paternity, which can be challenged through the judicial process. Teleconferencing has been allowed to present testimony in paternity actions, at the discretion of the court.

The state uses an expedited judicial process to establish its support orders. The state will allow a petition for support when the only issue is retroactive support.

The enforcement process is administrative and judicial. The trigger criterion for filing a lien is a one thousand five hundred dollar arrearage.

An IV-D case may be reviewed every three years or upon a substantial change of circumstance. Other cases are reviewed at the request of either party.

There must be a substantial change in circumstance to justify a modification. This would include a twenty percent increase or decrease in the income of either parent, extraordinary uninsured medical expenses, or that three years have elapsed since the date the last order was issued.

There are other criteria which can justify a modification of the order. These include 1) economic consequence of the presence of step-parents; step-children, or other natural or adoptive children; 2) reasonable expenses of exercising visitation; 3) economic consequences of the disposition of the marital home; 4) the federal tax consequences of the order; 5) state tax obligations; 6) split or shared custody arrangements; and 7) post secondary or secondary educational expenses of the children of the order or other children.

NEW JERSEY

The program is state administered and county operated. There is no statute of limitations as to past due child support.

New Jersey uses the shared income model to calculate child support. When the state issues an order establishing paternity, it will address issues of custody and visitation.

Marriage constitutes a presumption of paternity, which may be rebutted by clear and convincing evidence.

The presumption also occurs where the parents have been married, if a marriage was attempted prior to birth, or after birth and declared invalid; if the putative father openly holds the child out to be his, or provides support for the child; acknowledges paternity in writing and files such with the local registrar, provided this is not disputed by the natural mother.

The state uses a judicial process to establish the support obligation. The court will consider the parent's gross income and assets; prior support orders, child care costs; special medical needs of the child; and second family involvement. The court can deviate

306

from the guidelines based if the result is unjust or inappropriate. The state will not allow a petition for support where the only issue is retroactive support.

The enforcement mechanism is both administrative and judicial. A non-custodial parent has thirty days to challenge a freeze and seize action. The action can be vacated upon grounds including mistaken identity, incorrect arrearage amount, court litigation, joint account, and extreme hardship.

An IV-D case is reviewed every three years. Other cases are reviewed upon request. The criterion for modification is a twenty percent change in the existing order.

The circumstances which might justify a modification include increase or decrease in the earnings of either parent, change in the needs of a parent or child, or extraordinary uninsured medical expenses.

<u>NEW MEXICO</u>

The program is state administered and operated. There is a statute of limitations applicable to collection of past due support. The statute extends fourteen years from the date of judgment as to unpaid court ordered support.

New Mexico uses the shared income model to calculate child support. When the state enters an order establishing paternity, it does not address issues of custody and visitation. Marriage constitutes a presumption of paternity, rebuttable by the results of paternity tests. Testimony can be presented by telephonic appearance at paternity hearings.

The state process to establish a support obligation is exclusively judicial. The state will allow a petition for child support when the only issue is retroactive support.

In New Mexico, a child support obligation is considered a lien on real property. A non-custodial parent has fifteen days after receiving notice to challenge a freeze and seize action. The basis to do so can be incorrect delinquency balance or joint ownership.

An IV-D case is reviewed every three years. Other support cases are reviewed at the request of the custodial parent, the non-custodial parent, or automatically in TANF cases. The review is done by judicial hearing which addresses the issue of change of circumstances.

The basic criterion for modification is a twenty percent change from the current order up or down, and one year since the last change. Grounds can include increase or decrease in the income of either parent, change in the needs of a party or the child, extraordinary uninsured medical expenses, or a change in child care expenses.

Disability benefits paid on behalf of the custodial parent can offset his or her child support obligation within the discretion of the court.

<u>NEW YORK</u>

The program is administered by the state, and operated by the counties. There is an applicable statute of limitations as to the collection of past due child support. This extends for twenty years from the date of default in payment regardless of whether the past due amount has been reduced to judgment for support orders issued after 8/7/87. The statute extends six years from default on orders entered before 8/7/87. Finally, the statute extends twenty years for all defaults in payment which have been granted as a money judgment.

The state uses a hybrid model between a shared income and percentage of income model to calculate child support. The formula includes a "basic percentage of income component" and a "supplementary shared income component" with respect to supplemental costs such as child care, educational expenses, excess medical costs, and rent. A child of divorced parents should receive the same proportion of parental income that he or she would have received if the parents were together.

When the state issues an order establishing paternity, it will address issues of custody and visitation. Marriage does constitute a presumption of paternity, which is rebuttable. Telephonic and other electronic testimony is available for certain paternity cases.

The state uses a judicial process to establish a support obligation. In addition to the custodial and non-custodial parent, a new spouse's income can be considered in the calculation of child support. This can occur where the parties married in a community property jurisdiction and did not sign a contrary pre-nuptial agreement.

There are ten factors which can be considered in rebutted the result of the child support guidelines. These are 1) financial resources of both parents; 2) physical and emotional health of child and special needs and aptitudes; 3) standard of living the child would have enjoyed if the marriage or household had not dissolved; 4) tax consequences to the partiers; 5) non-monetary contributions to the care and well being of the child by either party; 7) educational needs of either parent; 8) a determination that the gross income of one parent is substantially higher than the other; 9) extraordinary

311

expense in exercising visitation; 10) and other factor the court deems relevant.

The state will not allow a petition for support where the only issue is retroactive support.

The trigger criterion for filing a lien is arrears greater than four months. The non-custodial parent has thirty days to challenge a freeze and seize action. The basis for challenge includes the fact that arrears are already paid, or that the money in the account belongs to a joint account holder.

An IV-D case is reviewed every two years. Other reviews are scheduled upon request of the parties. The grounds for judicial modification are that a substantial change of circumstances has occurred, or that the petitioner is unable to provide for the needs of the child and an increase is warranted based upon the best interests of the child.

For administrative review a cost of living adjustment is used. For an official modification of the order, a judicial review is required.

A specific change of circumstance must be detailed in the Uniform Support Petition.

For the cost of living increase, a minimum ten percent increase in the obligation is necessary to modify the order. For other petitions, there is no such criterion.

<u>NORTH CAROLINA</u>

The program is state administered and operated. The statute of limitations applicable to the collection of past due child support is ten years.

North Carolina uses the income shared model to calculate child support. When the state enters an order establishing paternity, it does not address issues of custody or visitation. Marriage constitutes a presumption of paternity, rebuttable by competent evidence. Written and teleconference evidence is commonly used in paternity hearings.

The state uses both an administrative and a judicial process to establish a support obligation. The administrative process is used when the non-custodial parent agrees and signs a voluntary support order and agreement. The income of the other biological parent is considered in calculating support if available. The state will allow a petition for support where the only issue is retroactive support.

The support enforcement process is administrative in nature. The trigger criterion for filing a lien is a three month arrearage or an

314

arrearage in excess of three thousand dollars. The non-custodial parent, or any affected account holder, has ten days after service of notice to challenge the action. The challenge can be based upon a legal exemption or a mistake in fact.

An IV-D case is reviewed every three years. In public assistance cases, reviews are automatic. In other cases, reviews are upon request of a party.

The criteria for modification of an existing order is a fifteen percent difference from the present order amount if the existing support order is three or more years old. If the order is less than three years old, there must be a showing of a "substantial change of circumstances."

The state considers numerous factors as to a request for modification, including change in the income of either parent, change in the needs of a parent or the child, extraordinary uninsured medical expense, or a change in day care costs, In addition, the court can consider the physical and emotional needs of the child, educational needs, change in costs relating to the age of

315

the child, the addition of other biological children, or a change in custody status of the child.

NORTH DAKOTA

The program is state administered and operated. There is no statute of limitations as to the collection of past due support, effective 4/2/1999. As to obligations incurred prior to that date, the statute of limitations only serves to bar certain judicial enforcement remedies. It does not extinguish the debt.

North Dakota calculates child support using a variable percentage of the non-custodial parent's net income. When the state issues an order establishing paternity, it does not address issues of custody and visitation. Marriage results in a presumption of paternity. A proceeding brought by a presumed father, mother, or other individual to adjudicate the paternity of a child having a presumed father must be commenced no later than two years after the child's birth. However, a proceeding to disprove paternity may be commenced at any time if the court finds that the parties did not cohabitate or engage in sexual intercourse during the probable time of conception. This is provided, however, that the presumed father never openly held the child out as his own.

A similar presumption is created if a man resides in the same household as a child for the first two years of life, and openly holds the child out as his own.

Written, video, and audio testimony is acceptable in a paternity hearing.

The state uses a judicial process to establish the support obligation. The state uses his income of the non-custodial parent only to calculate support, excluding means tested public assistance benefits, employee benefits over which the employee has no significant control and child support payments.

The presumptive guidelines can be rebutted upon a showing of various circumstances. These include increased need of support for more than six children, the increased ability to pay of the non-custodial parent with an income in excess of twelve thousand five hundred dollars per month to pay child support, educational costs incurred with the consent of the non-custodial parent, disability or illness of the child, increase in expense due to age of child, increased cost of child care, increased ability to pay due to assets owned by non-custodial parent, unusual expense incurred in

318

visitation, hardship of the non-custodial parent beyond his or her control, work or daily living expenses, health expenses of the non-custodial parent, the fact that a support calculation considers atypical overtime wages or bonuses, and a situation in which the income of the custodial parent is at least three times higher than the net income of the non-custodial parent.

The state will establish support orders for prior periods.

The enforcement process is administrative. A real property lien is automatically created when judgment for any amount of past due support is docketed. A personal property lien is created where past due support is greater than two times the current or most recent monthly support obligation, or two thousand dollars, whichever is less.

A non-custodial parent has thirty days to request a court review of an administrative lien. He or she also has ten days to file a claim for exemption with the sheriff of the county in which the party resides. The non-custodial parent also has ten days to challenge a child support deduction order.

An IV-D case is reviewed every three years. Other cases are reviewed upon the request of a party. The criterion for modification is a fifteen percent change upwards or downwards. The criteria for demonstrating a change in circumstance which would justify modification of a support order are not otherwise specifically defined.

<u>OHIO</u>

The program is state administered and operated. The state has no statute of limitations with regards to the collection of unpaid child support.

Ohio uses the income shares model to calculate child support. When the state enters an order establishing paternity, it does not address issues of custody and visitation. Marriage constitutes a presumption of paternity, which can be rebutted by a showing that the marriage did not actually occur. Telephone and other electronic means of testimony are permissible in a paternity action.

A child support order is established by judicial process. The income of a new spouse or a child's income may be used in a request for a deviation from the guidelines. There are several factors which might justify a deviation from the guidelines, including: extraordinary obligations for handicapped or disabled children who are not of the relationship from which the obligation is derived; other court ordered payments, obligor obtains additional employment after order issued in order to support a second family, financial resources and earning ability of child; disparity in income; benefits either party

321

receives from remarriage or cohabitation; effect of tax obligations; direct payments made by a parent outside of the court ordered obligation; standard of living the child would have had absent divorce or breakup of the family; needs of the child' educational needs of opportunities; responsibility of parent to support others; or any other relevant factor.

The state will not allow a child support action where only retroactive support is requested.

The enforcement process is by both administrative and judicial methods. The criteria for filing a lien is any delinquency of child support payments. The non-custodial parent has seven days to contest a freeze and seize action. A secondary account holder has ten days, and receives a separate notice of the seizure. The obligor cannot appeal once the account has been frozen.

An IV-D case is reviewed every thirty six months, unless there is a thirty percent change in gross income, projected to last six months, or removal of one child or more from the obligation due to emancipation or death. Other reviews are scheduled at the request of the parties.

The grounds for modification include increase or decrease in the income of a parent, extraordinary uninsured medical expense, or deletion of a child from the obligation due to emancipation, death, or incarceration.

OKLAHOMA

The program is state administered. There is no statute of limitations as to the collection of past due support.

Oklahoma uses the shared income model to calculate support. When the state enters an order establishing paternity, it does not address child custody or visitation.

Marriage constitutes a presumption of paternity. This may be rebutted by the filing of a petition within two years of the child's birth if the child is reared by the parents or a family member or by filing a denial of paternity form with an affidavit acknowledging paternity by the natural father. In paternity hearings testimony by telephone is usually allowed.

The state uses an administrative and a judicial process to establish an order of support. The administrative process is used more commonly. Support can be retroactive for a five year period in paternity cases and non-TANF cases only.

The enforcement process is administrative. Past due child support amounts become a line automatically by operation of law.

324

To trigger a freeze and seize action, arrears must equal the child support payable for at least ninety days. The non-custodial parent has ten days to request an administrative review.

An IV-D case is reviewed annually if the non-custodial parent is located, or at the request of the state agency. Other cases are reviewed upon request.

In the modification process, financial data is reviewed by the state agency. If a modification is appropriate, the agency attempts to obtain an agreement to same. If not, the parties have fifteen days to object to the recommendation, and submit evidence. A hearing date is then scheduled.

The trigger criteria for a modification is a change upwards or downwards of at least ten percent. The order can be modified for reasons including increase or decrease in the income of a party or the child, change in the needs of the child or a party, extraordinary uninsured medical expense, change in child care expenses, or that the order is not in compliance with the support guidelines, or visitation exceeds one hundred and twenty nights per year.

OREGON

The program is state administered, and operated by a jointly by the state and county. The applicable statute of limitations for collection of unpaid child support is ten years from date of accrual for payments due before 1/01/94. Any judgment entered after that date expires twenty five years from the date of the original judgment.

Oregon uses a shared income model to calculate child support. The state does not address issues of custody and visitation when establishing a paternity order. Marriage constitutes a rebuttable presumption of paternity. Oregon law does not recognize "conclusive" presumptions of paternity.

The enforcement mechanism is both administrative and judicial. The administrative process is used wherever possible. Income of a new spouse may be used as a rebuttal in a child support establishment proceeding. There are extensive grounds for deviation from the child support guidelines, which include hardship of either party, ability to borrow, extraordinary or diminished needs of the child, desirability of a custodial parent remaining in the home, the income of a spouse or domestic partner, evidence that the child is not living with either party and is not a "child attending school," or the return of capital.

Support enforcement in the state is an administrative process. Any arrearage is the trigger criterion for the filing of a lien. A minimum five hundred dollar delinquency and three months delinquent will result in the filing of a lien.

When the non-custodial parent is in Oregon, he or she has three months to challenge a freeze and seize action. The challenge can be based upon a property exemption or the fact that the asset is not owner by the non-custodial parent.

An IV-D case is reviewed every three years. Other cases are reviewed at the request of a party. The criteria for modification of a child support order is a fifty dollar a month change in the payment, or fifteen percent up or down, whichever is less.

Change of circumstance can also be shown by emancipation of a child; that the non-custodial parent is incarcerated with no known assets or income; parties reside together and are supporting the child; the child was not included in the original order; a change in physical custody has occurred; a new written agreement has changed parenting time; or a change in medical support has occurred.

PENNSYLVANIA

The program is state administered and county operated. There is no statute of limitations with regards to unpaid child support.

The state uses the income shares model to calculate support. The state does not address issues of custody and child support when it enters an order of paternity. Marriage results in a presumption of paternity, which can be rebutted by proof of lack of access, physical incapacity, or genetic test upon request. Written testimony and teleconference testimony are permitted in a paternity action.

The state uses both an administrative and a judicial process to establish a child support obligation. The administrative action is used when the matter is uncontested. The state will allow a petition for child support when the only issue is retroactive support.

Any child support arrearage can result in the filing of a lien. There is a specified amount of time for the non-custodial parent to be delinquent prior to proceeding with a freeze and seize action, which is thirty days. The non-custodial parent has thirty days to challenge such an action. The grounds for contest include the fact that no overdue support exists, that there is a mistake in the certified amount of support overdue, mistake in the identity of the obligor, or the account is exempt as a matter of law.

An IV-D case is reviewed every three years. Other cases are scheduled for review upon request. The petition for modification if filed with the court and a modification conference is scheduled. The requesting party must show a substantial change in circumstances.

The grounds for modification include increase or decrease in the income of either parent, change in the needs of a parent or children, extraordinary uninsured medical expense, or change in child care expenses.

RHODE ISLAND

The program is state administered and operated. There is no statute of limitations for the collection of past due child support.

Rhode Island uses the income shares model to calculate a child support obligation. When the state issues an order establishing paternity, it does not address issues of custody and visitation.

The support enforcement mechanism is administrative. The trigger criterion for filing a lien is five hundred dollars or more arrearage. The state does not issue bank levies unless the non-custodial parent has received notice of the child support debt within the past twelve months, there is a valid court order, and any of the following criteria exist:

Arrears, interest, and penalty of one thousand five hundred dollars or more, or the non-custodial parent has failed to make any "non-enforcement payments" in the prior six weeks. The non-custodial parent has thirty days to contest a freeze and seize action.

A non-debtor has the same rights as the non-custodial parent.

A title IV-D case is reviewed every three years, upon request. Other cases are reviewed upon request of either parent or the state where applicable. The criterion for modification is a ten percent change in the obligation, upwards or downwards. This is noted by the state as "a guide."

The possible reasons for modification include increase or decrease in the income of either parent, change in the needs of a parent or child, extraordinary uninsured medical expense, or substantial change in child care expenses.

SOUTH CAROLINA

The program is state administered and operated. There is no statute of limitations with regards to the collection of past due support, but title IV-D cases will not be established after the child reaches the age of eighteen.

South Carolina uses the income shares model to calculate support. When the state issues an order establishing paternity, it does not address issues of custody or child support. Marriage constitutes a presumption of paternity, rebuttable in a family court proceeding.

A support order may be established by an administrative or judicial process. The administrative process is used more commonly. The judicial process is used in contested cases.

The criterion for deviating from the child support guidelines is at the discretion of the court. The trigger criterion for filing a lien is an arrearage of one thousand dollars or more. The non-custodial parent has thirty days to challenge a freeze and seize action.

The grounds for contest include incorrect obligor, or incorrect arrearage amount.

An IV-D case is reviewed every three years. Other cases are reviewed at the request of either party. The modification process is judicial in nature.

The trigger criterion for modification is a twenty percent change, up or down, from the present order. The grounds for change include increase or decrease in the income of either parent, change in the needs of a parent or child, extraordinary uninsured medical expenses, or change in child care expenses.

SOUTH DAKOTA

The program is state administered and operated. The statue of limitations for the collection of past due support is twenty years from the date support is due.

South Dakota uses the income shares model to calculate child support. When the state enters an order establishing paternity, it does not address issues of custody or child support. Marriage constitutes a presumption of paternity. To rebut the presumption, either party must file a challenge to the affidavit of paternity in circuit court within sixty days. A party can also contest paternity for a period of up to three years after signing the paternity affidavit on the basis of fraud, duress, or material mistake of fact. In order to do so, it is necessary to file an action in circuit court.

To establish paternity, the father must either sign an affidavit of paternity, or a genetic test must determine same to a ninety nine percent probability, or there must be a judgment of paternity by the circuit court. Videotape and teleconferencing can be used to present testimony in a paternity hearing, at the discretion of the court.

The support order is established by an administrative and judicial process. The judicial process is used in contested actions. The state will allow a petition for support where retroactive support is the sole issue, limited to three years from the date of the application.

The enforcement process is administrative. Any arrearage is the trigger criteria for filing a lien. The minimum dollars amount that the non-custodial parent must be delinquent prior to becoming eligible for asset seizure is one thousand dollars

If the account subject to seizure is a joint account, the minimum amount of money which must be in the account to become eligible for seizure is five thousand dollars.

The parties have twenty days from the date the payment received by the State Disbursement Unit to challenge a freeze and seize action. A second contest to a freeze and seize action is possible if a request if filed within ten days.

An IV-D case is reviewed every three years. Other cases are reviewed upon request. The process involves submission of

336

evidence to the state agency, who submits a recommendation to the court. If objections are filed, a hearing in scheduled as to the issue of modification. If not, the court enters the modified order.

The trigger criteria for modification is an increase or decrease in the amount of the obligation of twenty percent or more,

The grounds for modification include increase or decrease in the income of either parent, change in the needs of either parent or child, extraordinary uninsured medical expenses, or change in child care costs.

TENNESSEE

The program is state administered and operated. There is no statute of limitations as to the collection of unpaid child support.

Tennessee uses the income shares model to calculate child support. When the state issues an order establishing paternity, it does not address issues of custody of visitation. Marriage constitutes a presumption of paternity, which is rebuttable. This can be done when all parties sign an affidavit as to the identity of the natural father through a court action. The presumption also applies if the child is born within ten months of the date of divorce or dissolution of marriage.

In an action to establish paternity, the court will usually rely upon the standard paternity affidavit. However, interrogatories may be used, as well as written, videotaped, or teleconferenced testimony. This is at the discretion of the court.

The state lien process is both administrative and judicial. The trigger criterion for filing a lien is an arrearage of five hundred dollars or more. There is no set time for the non-custodial parent to be delinquent to trigger the filing of a lien. The non-custodial parent has fifteen days to challenge a freeze and seize action.

The grounds for challenge include the correctness of the identity of the person against whom the action is directed; a mistake in fact involving the action of the department; correctness of the amount of the obligation; the extent of the non-custodial parent's interest in the asset; and whether good cause exists to not seize, sell, levy upon, distribute, or otherwise dispose of all or part of the asset.

TEXAS

The program is state operated and administered. There is a jurisdictional limitation after termination of the child support obligation, with an effect comparable to a statute of limitations. The limitation is ten years for enforcement of a judgment and six months for a contempt of court action.

Texas uses fixed shares of income model to calculate child support, with adjustment for multiple family obligations. The court may grant a variance from the guidelines in its discretion.

When the state issues an order establishing paternity, it will address issues of custody and visitation. This occurs in intrastate cases only. A presumption of joint managing conservatorship is considered to be in the child's best interest. A "standard" visitation schedule is followed.

Marriage constitutes a presumption of paternity. This is rebuttable by an adjudication which must be done before the fourth birthday of the child; except where it can be shown that the presumed father and mother did not live together or engage in sexual intercourse during the probable period of conception; and the presumed father never held the child out to be his own.

There are other facts which can lead to a presumption of legitimacy. This occurs if the party and the biological mother are or have been married to each other and the child is born less than three hundred days from the date of divorce or dissolution; the mother

and the party attempted a marriage within three hundred days of the date of the child's birth; the party has filed a written acknowledgment of paternity of the child; he voluntarily is named the father on the birth certificate; he is obliged to support the child through a written, voluntary promise; during the first two years of his life, he continuously resided with the child and held the child out to be his own.

The support order is established by a quasi-administrative process. The judicial process is used where a party is presently incarcerated, there is a history of family violence, foster care, a minor party, the custodial party is not the mother or father, when a presumed father needs to be excluded, or contempt is sought.

341

The criterion for rebutting the child support guidelines includes the fact that the application of the guidelines would be unjust and inappropriate.

As to the issue of retroactive support, if the child is not emancipated, current support will be sought along with the retroactive support. The retroactive period will be four years unless the custodial parent has waived the right to any unassigned retroactive support. The calculating retroactive support, the court shall consider the relevant time period and 1) whether there has been any attempt to notify the biological father of his paternity; 2) whether the biological father had knowledge of his probable or actual paternity; 3) whether the retroactive order will cause undue hardship upon the biological father and his family; 4) whether the biological father has provided actual support or other necessities prior to the filing of the action.

The enforcement process is judicial. There is no requirement that the non-custodial parents receives notice of a freeze and seize action. The criteria for such an action is any amount of past due support. However, the non-custodial has ten days to challenge a levy (i.e. a freeze and seize action.)

The lien must be release if there was a mistake in identity, or if there is an absence of arrears.

An IV-D case is reviewed every three years. Other cases are also reviewed every three years or at the request of a party. The general standard for modification is a substantial change of circumstances that has occurred since the date of the order. This would generally occur where the amount of child support to be awarded differs twenty percent or one hundred dollars a month, upwards or downwards.

The grounds for modification include an increase or decrease in the income of the non-custodial parent, a change in the needs of a parent or the child, extraordinary uninsured medical expense, or change in child care expenses.

UTAH

The program is state administered and operated. There is an applicable statute of limitations with regards to unpaid child support. This extends from the majority of the last child named in the order, plus four years unless a sum certain judgment has been obtained. In case of a judgment, an eight year statute of limitations from the date of the judgment applies.

Utah uses an income shares model to calculate child support. The state does not address issues of custody or visitation when issuing an order establishing paternity. Marriage constitutes a presumption of paternity, rebuttable by court action or genetic test results.

The support order is established by a primarily administrative process. The judicial process is used where no prior judicial order exists, or a prior judicial order authorizes use of the administrative process. The judicial process is most frequently used where there is a minor parent.

The grounds for rebutting the use of the child support guidelines related to the result being unjust or inappropriate, or the result not being in the best interest of the child.

The state will allow a petition for support where the only issue is retroactive support, but not when the child is already emancipated.

The support enforcement process is administrative. The trigger criterion for filing a lien is an arrearage of one hundred and fifty dollars in a TANF case, or five hundred dollars in a non-TANF case.

The non-custodial parent must be delinquent by sixty days in the obligation to permit the use of a freeze and seize action. There is a time period of fifteen days during which the non-custodial parent may challenge the action.

The grounds for challenge include the fact that the case is under administrative review, some or all funds are subject to an exemption, some or all funds do not belong to the obligor, or that the obligor is contesting the amount of the arrearage.

An IV-D case is reviewed every three years, or as requested. Other cases are reviewed at the request of a party or the state.

Income information is gathered and the state guidelines are applied. Modification is pursued when the amount of change meets the statutory threshold. The threshold is ten percent change in the payment, upwards or downwards, if it has been three years since the last order date. The criterion is a substantial change of circumstances and a change of fifteen percent, if the previous order is less than three years old.

VERMONT

The system is state administered and operated. There is an applicable statute of limitations with regards to unpaid child support. In cases with an order, but no adjudicated arrearage, an action to adjudicate arrears must be taken within six yeas after the youngest child reaches eighteen years of age. In case in which the issue of arrears has been previously adjudicated, the limit is eight years from the date of the last adjudication.

Vermont uses the shared income model to calculate child support. When the state issues an order establishing paternity, the court will address issues of custody and visitation. Marriage constitutes a presumption of paternity. It is rebuttable by challenge, but only by a showing of mistake, inadvertence, excusable neglect, newly discovered evidence, or fraud. There is also a presumption of paternity based upon failure to submit to genetic testing as ordered without good cause, provided that the court finds a probability that the party is the biological father.

The support order establishment process is judicial. Both the income of the mother and the non-custodial parent are considered.

347

Deviation is possible based upon numerous factors, including hardship and unfair result. To obtain an order of retroactive support, the custodial parent must show that the non-custodial parent had knowledge of the child, and custodial parent made a diligent effort to establish paternity.

The support enforcement process is administrative. The trigger criteria for a lien is that the judgment is thirty days old or older, with no appeal pending, and the debt is greater than 1/12th of the annual obligation.

The state requires that a minimum amount of money be in a bank account to be eligible for a freeze and seize action. The amount is seven hundred dollars in a savings account, two thousand dollars in a checking account, and a retirement account in excess of five thousand three hundred dollars. The non-custodial parent has twenty days from the date of service of the notice to contest a freeze and seize action.

A TANF cased is reviewed every three years. Other cases are reviewed at any time at the request of a party.

The procedure is judicial. The party making the request has the burden of proof, and must show real, substantial, and unanticipated change of circumstances. A ten percent change in the amount of the obligation, upwards or downwards, three years without review, or the receipt of unemployment compensation, worker's compensation, or disability benefits constitutes grounds for modification.

The criteria for modification further include an increase or decrease in the income of either parent, a change in the needs of a parent or child, extraordinary medical expenses not covered by insurance, or change in the costs of child care.

VIRGINIA

The program is state administered and operated. There is no statute of limitations applicable to unpaid child support.

Virginia uses the income shares model to calculate child support. When the state issues an order establishing paternity, it does not address issues of custody or visitation.

Marriage constitutes a presumption of paternity, rebuttable by a showing of reasonable doubt at an adjudicatory hearing.

The support order is established through an administrative process with a judicial backup. The administrative process is preferred by the state, with the judicial process used in cases involving a minor parent, incarcerated felons, or after the administrative process has been exhausted. The state will allow a petition for support where the only issue is retroactive support. However, Virginia will not establish support for prior periods except for the repayment of public assistance debt.

Further, no debt can be established where the public assistance was paid before the putative father was determined to be

350

the legal father, or for a period in which the non-custodial parent received public assistance or SSI, had no verified identifiable assets, or was institutionalized, incarcerated, or totally and permanently disabled.

The enforcement process is administrative and judicial. The trigger criterion for filing a lien is arrears equal or exceeding five hundred dollars or evidence that the non-custodial parent owns real or personal property.

The non-custodial parent has ten days to contest a freeze and seize action. He or she has a further right to file a "de-novo" appeal within ten days of receiving notice of the administrative hearing officer's decision in the initial appeal

A TANF case is reviewed every thirty six months. Other child support cases are reviewed at the request of either party.

The state modification procedure is triggered by a request in writing, which results in a judicial hearing. A difference in amount of ten percent upwards or downwards from the previous amount constitutes a substantial change which will permit modification of the order.

The grounds for modification can include an increase or decrease in the income of either party, change in the needs of a parent or child, extraordinary uninsured medical expenses, or change in child care expense.

WASHINGTON

The program is state administered and operated. For orders past due after 7/23/89, all past due support expires ten years after the eighteenth birthday of the youngest child named in the support order. For orders entered before that date, each monthly installment expires ten years after that monthly installment becomes due.

Washington uses the income shares model to calculate support. When the state issues an order establishing paternity, it will address issues of child support and custody. Marriage constitutes a presumption of paternity, rebuttable by court order, filed paternity acknowledgement, and the presumed father's denial of paternity. Written testimony is allowed at a paternity hearing.

The support order can be established by an administrative or a judicial process. The administrative process is used where paternity is not an issue and there is no court order either relieving the non-custodial parent of his obligation to support the child.

In setting the amount of support, the court will consider the income of any member of either household.

353

The trigger criterion for filing a lien is an arrearage of five hundred dollars or more. The non-custodial parent has twenty days to appeal a freeze and seize action. A non-debtor who is affected by such an action likewise has twenty days to appeal.

An IV-D case is reviewed every three years. Other cases are reviewed upon request.

The criteria for modification of an order is a change upwards or downwards of twenty five percent in the payment or one hundred dollars per month; or two thousand four hundred dollars over the life of the order.

The remaining stated grounds for modification in a substantial change in child care expenses.

<u>WEST VIRGINIA</u>

The program is state administered and operated. The statute of limitation for the collection of back child support is ten years from the date the last child covered under the order is emancipated.

West Virginia uses the income shares model to calculate child support. When the state issues an order establishing paternity, it does not address issues of custody and visitation. Marriage constitutes a presumption of paternity, rebuttable by court order under certain specified circumstances.

These include instances where 1) paternity has been determined otherwise by a court; 2) genetic testing is conclusive as to another biological father, or 3) cases in which the mother, husband, and biological father all acknowledge that the husband is not the father of the child. This evidence must be presented by properly executed affidavits.

Paternity can not be proved in this manner when the name of the husband appears on the birth certificate. Further, the affidavits and a genetic test must be completed and served upon the state agency within one year.

The support establishment process is judicial in nature. There are various grounds for a deviation from the child support guidelines, which include 1) Special needs of the child or support obligor, including the needs of an adult child who is physically or mentally disabled; 2) educational expense for a child or parent; 3) families with more than six children; 3) long distance visitation costs; 4) the child resides with a third party;

5) needs of another child or children to whom the custodial parent owes a duty of support; 6) the extent to which the non-custodial parent relies upon nonrecurring or nonguaranteed income; 7) whether the total amount of alimony, child support, and child care costs subtracted from the income of the non-custodial parent reduces his or her income to below the federal poverty level.

The support enforcement process is administrative. The trigger criterion for filing a lien is fourteen days delinquent, whole or partial payments, for personal property. For real property, the criteria is thirty days in arrears.

The state will not seize assets until arrears equal one month's support. The grounds to contest a freeze and seize action include mistaken identity, no ownership rights in the property, debt not owed, or that the account in question contains SSI funds.

An IV-D case is reviewed every three years. Other cases are reviewed where at least thirty six months have elapsed since the establishment or modification of the previous order, a request for review has been forwarded, or the case was previously selected for review, but closed because there was no employer.

A fifteen percent variance from the previous order is grounds for modification. The criteria for modification include a change in the income of the custodial or non-custodial parent, a change in the needs of a parent or the child, extraordinary uninsured medical expense, or a substantial change in day care costs.

<u>WISCONSIN</u>

The program is state administered and operated. The statute of limitations for the collection of unpaid child support is twenty years after the child or children reach the age of majority.

Wisconsin uses the percentage of income standard to calculate child support. When the state issues an order of paternity, it will address issues of child custody or support. Marriage constitutes a presumption of paternity, rebuttable by appointment of a guardian ad litem and genetic tests excluding the husband or by genetic tests showing ninety nine percent probabilities that another man is the father, even without locating the husband. The presumption also applies to marriage after the birth of the child.

The process of establishing the support obligation is judicial. There are sixteen factors which constitute criteria for deviation from the child support guidelines. These include 1) the financial resources of both parents and the child; 2) the needs of any person other than the child, who either parent is obligated to support, 3) the standard of living the child would have enjoyed if not for dissolution of the marriage or family; 4) the desirability of the custodial parent

358

remaining as a stay at home parent; 5) the cost of day care; 6) extraordinary travel expenses related to visitation; 7) the needs of the child related to health care costs; 8) the tax consequences to each party; 9) the best interests of the child; 10) the earning capacity of both parents; 11) any other factors the court deems relevant.

The support enforcement mechanism is administrative. The trigger criteria for filing a lien is five hundred dollars or one month's support, whichever is greater. The non-custodial parent must be one thousand dollars delinquent or delinquent by three hundred percent of the monthly payment to trigger an asset seizure.

WYOMING

The program is state administered. It is operated by a combination of private vendors and various aspects of county government. There is no statute of limitations as to the collection of past due child support.

The state calculates child support by using a percentage of the income of both parties. When the state issues an order establishing paternity, it does not address issues of custody or visitation.

Marriage constitutes a presumption of paternity, rebuttable by adjudication or acknowledgement.

The process of support order establishment is judicial. A deviation from the child support guidelines can be granted where the presumptive child support obligation is unjust or inappropriate for a particular situation. Retroactive support is not allowed if the child is emancipated. Prior support is limited to the ability to pay.

The trigger criteria for filing a lien is an arrearage equal to three times the monthly support obligation. The non-custodial parent has twenty business days from the date of the notice to contact the child support office to challenge a freeze and seize action.

An IV-D action is reviewed every three months. Other cases are reviewed upon the request of either party or the state.

The process requires that both parties complete a financial declaration and provide financial information. The issue is then resolved in a judicial hearing.

A twenty percent change in the presumptive support amount or substantial change in circumstances will permit a modification of an order. If the order is three years old, no change in the support amount or change of circumstances need be shown.

The criteria for modification include increase or decrease in the income of either parent, change in the needs of a parent or the child, extraordinary uninsured medical expenses, or substantial change in child care costs.

About the Author

Robert W. Rushing, Jr. is an attorney who has practiced law in South Carolina for over twenty years. His previous book, "Child Support: Representing the Non-Custodial Parent", was published by the South Carolina Bar in 2010, and is the only guide to this area of practice currently available to attorneys. He is also the co-host of a syndicated radio program, "Big Law.", and an adjunct professor at Francis Marion University in Florence, South Carolina.

www.ingramcontent.com/pod-product-compliance
Lightning Source LLC
Chambersburg PA
CBHW071355170526
45165CB00001B/56